THE MAKING OF A BRIDE

THE MAKING OF A BRIDE

THE SONG OF SOLOMON

VOLUME I: CHAPTERS 1:1—5:1

TWELVE STEPS
FROM FRIEND TO BRIDE OF CHRIST

DR. RONALD E. COTTLE

The Making of a Bride: The Song of Solomon
"Twelve Steps From Friend to Bride of Christ"

© 2016 Dr. Ronald E. Cottle

This book or parts thereof may not be reproduced in any form, stored in a retrieval system, or transmitted in any form by any means—electronic, mechanical, photocopy, recording, or otherwise—without prior written permission of the publisher, except as provided by United States copyright law.

Unless otherwise quoted, all Scripture quotations are from the Holy Bible, King James Version (KJV).

Scripture quotations marked NKJV are from the Holy Bible, New King James Version. Copyright © 1982, Thomas Nelson, Inc.

Scripture quotations marked NIV are from the Holy Bible, New International Version. Copyright © 1973, 1978, 1984, International Bible Society.

Scripture quotations and marginal notes marked ERV, taken from the Easy-to-Read Version of the Bible, Copyright © 2006 by Bible League International, World Bible Translation Center, Atlanta, GA. Used by permission, All rights reserved..

Scriptures marked NLT are taken from The Holy Bible, New Living Translation, copyright © 1996. Used by permission of Tyndale House Publishers, Inc., Wheaton, Illinois 60189. All rights reserved.

Scripture quotations marked NASV are from New American Standard Bible Copyright © 1960, 1962, 1963, 1968, 1971, 1972, 1973, 1975, 1977, by The Lockman Foundation. Used by permission. All rights reserved.

Scripture quotations marked MSG are taken from THE MESSAGE® Copyright © 1993,1994,1995, 1996, 2000, 2001, 2002. Used by Permission of NavPress Publishing Group. Colorado springs, CO. All rights reserved.

Scripture quotations marked ASV are taken from the American Stantard Version of the Bible. It is in the public domain.

First Edition – March 2016 – Printed in the United States of America

ISBN: 978-1-941453-14-8

REC Ministries
6003 Veterans Parkway
Columbus, GA 31909

Phone: (706) 256-0100   Fax: (706) 653-0487
www.roncottleministries.com

O my dove, that art in the clefts of the rock, **in the secret places of the stairs***, let me see thy countenance, let me hear thy voice; for sweet is thy voice, and thy countenance is comely.*

(Song of Solomon 2:14)

Table of Contents

Introduction ix

STAGE A - FROM PERFORMANCE TO OBEDIENCE

The First Stairstep – Saved and Obedient
Chapter 1 – Friend 3

The Second Stairstep – Hungry for More
Chapter 2 – God-Chaser 11

The Third Stairstep – Experiences of Intimacy
Chapter 3 – Lover 25

STAGE B – FROM TRANSPARENT RELATIONSHIP TO SURRENDER

The Fourth Stairstep – Fairest Among Women
Chapter 4 – Experiences to Relationship 45
Chapter 5 – The Well-beloved's Instructions 53
Chapter 6 – The King's Table 71

The Fifth Stairstep – Communion with Him – Dove
Chapter 7 – Devoted 77

The Sixth Stairstep – Surrender to Him – Separated
Chapter 8 – Vulnerable 103

STAGE C - FROM SECLUDED COMPANIONSHIP TO WEDDING PROCESSIONAL

The Seventh Stairstep – Secluded with Him
Chapter 9 – Betrothed (Chosen to Wed, Companion) 119
Chapter 10 - Betrothed (Valley of Trouble) 133

The Eighth Stairstep – Union with Him
Chapter 11 – Espoused (Legally Engaged) 147

The Ninth Stairstep – Transfigured by Him

Chapter 12 – Transported to the Wedding (Processional) 159

STAGE D – FROM WEDDING PREPARATION TO BRIDE AND PARTNER

The Tenth Stairstep – Exalted by Him

Chapter 13 – Prepared and Exalted for the Wedding (Ready) ... 179
Chapter 14 – The New Creation in Christ 185

The Eleventh Stairstep – Seated in the Heavens with Him

Chapter 15 - Enthroned (Established) 205

The Twelfth Stairstep – Serving Others with Him

Chapter 16 – Bride (Partner) 217

About the Author 243

INTRODUCTION

THE SONG OF SOLOMON…

Is it simply mystic and erotic Near Eastern literature from 3,000 years ago? Or is it a majestic mix of difficult religious images and unrelated Jewish love poems?

When was the last time you heard a message or read a book on the Song of Solomon?

Let me tell you a secret: Most preachers and theologians carefully avoid the Song, simply because they don't understand the book. They dread the prospect of teaching from a book filled with so many hard-to-explain phrases and intimate sexual references.

Frankly, many of the newer books written about The Song of Solomon deeply disappoint me. Many interpreters follow a modern fad that arbitrarily rejects allegory and parable as useless teaching tools (someone should have notified Jesus about this). The "new and improved" method interprets the Song primarily as a kind of erotic sex manual.

I feel they have totally missed the true power of this most misunderstood of all books in the biblical canon. Remember that the finest and most valued treasures on earth tend to be buried deep in rock, or require diligence and hard labor to unearth them and present them to the world.

This is also true of the "true riches" embedded deeply within the Bible, only it takes more than diligence and hard labor to harvest spiritual treasure. It takes supernatural help from the Holy Spirit of God.

Allow the Holy Spirit to transform the Song of Solomon from "a book that has baffled scholars and religious leaders for thousands of years" into a "divine stairway to deeper relationship with Jesus Christ, the Bridegroom of the Ages."

I was one of those who really didn't feel comfortable with the Song of Solomon until God assigned the Song to me after I had a painful accident on a runaway scooter and a steep incline several years ago.

Then an emergency hospital visit turned into a number of days of mandatory bed rest. When I asked the Lord to help me make the most of that painful time, He led me to launch an in-depth study of the Song of Solomon. (He had finally made me "sit still" long enough to tackle a project I'd avoid otherwise.)

The Song came alive to me as never before in nearly five decades of scholarly study, pastoral ministry, and academic teaching.

The Holy Spirit revealed twelve vital stairsteps of divine relationship concealed within the first four chapters of the Song.

These stages transport followers of Christ from the first step of friendship all the way to the twelfth step of union with Him as part of His corporate "sister-bride" at the wedding supper of the Lamb!

Each step will amaze you, and the details of the journey will answer and explain important questions you've had about your life, your trials, and even some of the deep frustrations you've felt along the way.

As you progress through this book and the Song of Solomon, expect your faith to expand and your excitement and love for Christ Jesus to blossom as never before.

I pray *The Making of a Bride* will strengthen your faith, sharpen your hunger for God and His Word, and equip you to press on in your journey through life with the Beloved, Jesus Christ!

Dr. Ronald E. Cottle
Columbus, Georgia
February, 2016

THE MAKING OF A BRIDE
"THE ROCK-STAIRS"
of
THE SONG OF SOLOMON

STAGE A			STAGE B		
EXPERIENCES			RELATIONSHIPS		
I	II	III	IV	V	VI
SAVED by Him	HUNGER for Him	CHAMBER EXPERIENCES with Him	RELATIONSHIP with Him	COMMUNION with Him	SURRENDER to Him
FRIEND (Peaceful)	GOD–CHASER (Hungry)	LOVE (Intimate)	FAIREST AMONG WOMEN (Transparent)	DOVE (Devoted)	SEPARATED (Vulnerable)
1:1 (1 verse)	1:2–4a (2½ verses)	1:4b–6 (2½ verses)	1:7–14 (8 verses)	1:15–2:7 (11 verses)	2:8–13 (6 verses)

TWELVE STAIRSTEPS TO BECOME "THE BRIDE OF CHRIST"

	STAGE C			STAGE D		
	LEGAL			WEDDING		
VII	VIII	IX	X	XI	XII
SECLUDED with Him	UNION with Him	TRANSFIGURED by Him	EXALTED by Him	SEATED IN THE HEAVENS with Him	SERVING OTHERS with Him
BETROTHED Chosen to Wife (Companion)	ESPOUSED (Legally Engaged)	TRANSPORTED to the WEDDING (Processional)	PREPARED for the WEDDING (Ready)	ENTHRONED (Established)	BRIDE (Partner)
2:14 – 3:3 (7 verses)	3:4 – 5 (2 verses)	3:6 – 11 (6 verses)	4:1 – 5 (5 verses)	4:6 – 8 (3 verses)	4:9 – 5:1 (9 verses)

STAGE A

EXPERIENCES

FROM PERFORMANCE TO EXPERIENCE

The First Stairstep – Saved and Obedient
Chapter 1 – Friend

The Second Stairstep – Hungry for More
Chapter 2 – God-Chaser

The Third Stairstep – Experiences of Intimacy
Chapter 3 – Lover

Chapter 1

STAIRSTEP 1
FRIEND

SAVED AND OBEDIENT

Ye are my friends, if ye do the things which I command you.
(John 15:14)

Nearly 3,000 years ago, the wisest man on earth penned an elaborate love poem under the inspiration of God. We have struggled to understand this poem ever since.

Solomon, the king of Israel and the son of David, describes the growing relationship between two primary characters: the Beloved (the bridegroom) and a young woman he first calls "fairest among women."

J. Hudson Taylor, founder of the China Inland Mission, said this in his book, *Union and Communion*:

"The Song of Solomon is designed to lead the believer into the 'green pastures' of the Good Shepherd, thence to the 'banqueting house' (chambers of intimacy) of the King, and thence to the service of the 'vineyard' (ministry)...."[1]

Taylor wrote these words more than 100 years ago, hinting at the simple key that transformed the Song of Solomon from a Bible book I quietly avoided (and really didn't understand) into a wisdom-packed guide to spiritual maturity in Christ!

THE MAKING OF A BRIDE

The truths Hudson Taylor gleaned from the Song of Solomon were embodied in Taylor's ministry as a pioneer missionary working in China.[2]

King Solomon penned The Song in 950 B.C., but despite the nearly 3,000 year time span, this book transformed *my life* as well. Its secrets can transform the life of *every* believer who is determined to follow in the footsteps of Jesus Christ, the Son of God and divine Bridegroom.

During my enforced in-house recuperation from an accident, I found a vital key to unlock the wonders of Solomon's masterpiece in Song 2:14:

> *O my dove, that art in the clefts of the rock,* **in the secret places of the stairs***, let me see thy countenance, let me hear thy voice; for sweet is thy voice, and thy countenance is comely.*
> (Song of Solomon 2:14, emphasis added)

Working from the principle of "the secret places of the stairs" in this key passage, I began a detailed study of the first four chapters of the Song of Solomon. Referring often to the original Hebrew, I found *twelve steps* we must take in our individual journeys to "become the Bride."

The Song of Solomon appears to be several love poems describing the progression of a young Shulamite woman's relationship with her Beloved until she ultimately became what Solomon called his "sister-bride."

I found *12 stages* that directly *parallel* our path to maturity and intimacy with Jesus as members of the Bride of Christ.[3,4,5]

I am not the first to see stages of development in The Song that parallel the Christian life. In addition to J. Hudson Taylor, I read

CHAPTER 1 – FRIEND

A.B. Simpson's insights in *Loving As Jesus Loves*. He divided the Song into six sections:

"The Waiting Days" (1:2—2:7), "The Wooing Days" (2:8—3:5), "The Wedding Days" (3:6—5:1), "The Testing Days" (5:2—8:1), "Home Longings" (8:2-4), and "Homecoming" (8:5-14).[6]

L.D. Johnson, on the other hand, divided the Song into a series of *love poems*. He provides *three invaluable guidelines* that will help you and me as we go through the love poems in the Song together:

1. They are about the *love* of one Person for another: the Risen Lord's passionate love for *you!*

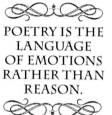
POETRY IS THE LANGUAGE OF EMOTIONS RATHER THAN REASON.

2. They are "poetry." Poetry is the language of the emotions rather than reason. Poetry intends to elicit an emotional response, not just a rational one.

3. They may not be understood apart from the gift of *imagination*. Its fullest meanings are always concealed and revealed only in symbol.[8]

Johnson maintained that the entire Song of Solomon is allegorical and everything in it is figurative. The primary characters, even though they are rooted in the literal figures of King Solomon and his Shulamite bride, represent the Risen Christ and the Redeemed Soul.

The traditional view among Jewish scholars is that the "Shulamite" was Abishag the Shunammite (1 Kings 1:3-4), the young virgin woman brought to the aged King David before his death (to keep him warm). Since David was not intimate with her, they feel she later became King Solomon's wife. Meanwhile, Solomon represented the resurrected David.

THE MAKING OF A BRIDE

I'm convinced, along with many other scholars, that the Shulamite represents the redeemed Christian on the journey to maturity and intimacy with the Lord. Solomon represents the Risen Christ; while the virgins (the only other major players in the drama of The Song of Solomon) represent the Church. Let's begin the journey through this amazing prophetic love poem penned by Solomon.

SOLOMON PREFIGURED JESUS IN HIS RISEN, GLORIFIED STATE.

Although the first verse of the Song of Songs declares it is *Solomon's* song, something much greater is afoot.

As we begin to trace the journey of the "virgin-hidden one" and the Beloved, we must understand we are also tracing the progress of *the soul* with the Risen Lord.

J. Hudson Taylor said, "Read without the 'key,' this book (the Song of Solomon) is specially unintelligible, but that key is easily found in the express teachings of the New Testament."[9]

> *God, who at sundry times and in divers manners spake in time past unto the fathers by the prophets,*
>
> *Hath in these last days spoken unto us by* **His Son**, *whom He hath appointed heir of all things, by whom also He made the worlds;*
>
> *Who being the brightness of His glory, and the express image of His person, and upholding all things by the word of His power, when He had by Himself purged our sins, sat down on the right hand of the Majesty on high.*
>
> (Hebrews 1:1-3, KJV, emphasis mine)

This passage glorifies Jesus for having completed His work of redemption as the "first begotten of the dead." It tells us He then sat down at the right hand of the Majesty on high.

CHAPTER 1 – FRIEND

(The Song of Solomon also glorifies Christ in His victory. Jewish scholars and teachers do not see the Song of Songs this way, but to this Christian writer and many others, *the Song makes little sense unless viewed through the "lens" of Christ Jesus, the Key of David.*)

It is significant that the Bible says the Song is "Solomon's song." In the Song, Solomon is "David resurrected," the king and bridegroom of Israel in her greatest days. Many believe that Israel under Solomon's rule represents her "Golden Age."

So what does this mean to you and to me?

The Song of Solomon represents the "song" of *Jesus*, the "greater David" and the Heavenly Bridegroom. He "sings" over every soul that is a developing member of His Bride (named in Revelation 21:2,9). The *individual* application of the Song is rooted in the key that Solomon (the Beloved in the Song) represents *the Risen Jesus!*

This Song is His Song in His Bride as she is gradually made one in heart with Him. In fact, this Song is echoed in every Bridal-Soul:

> *And they sung as it were a new song before the throne, and before the four beasts, and the elders: and no man could learn that song but the hundred and forty and four thousand, which were redeemed from the earth.* (Revelation 14:3, emphasis mine)

When this passage refers to the "elders" before the throne of God, it includes the 12 Patriarchs of Israel in the Old Testament *and* the 12 apostles of the New Testament.

This song of the Alpha and the Omega, the Beginning and the End, is to be sung throughout eternity! Some scholars believe that even the numbers used portray "*Christ prefigured* in the Old Testament times *Christ revealed* and risen in the New Testament = Infinity."[10]

Although Solomon penned the Song of Songs nearly 3,000 years ago, the Lord uses it *today* to reveal the *heart-history* of every redeemed soul who is led on a journey to know the Lord.

This is how the Bridegroom from Heaven *woos*[11] the soul on earth for whom He died and rose again!

Step into this miraculous twelve-stage journey as Christ the Bridegroom draws the Bride into His own life, "who was declared to be the Son of God with power ... by the resurrection of the dead" (Romans 1:4).

Our earliest stage in *the surrendered life* as Believers is marked by the name, Friend, or "love companion," from Song of Solomon 1:9: "I have compared thee, O my love [*rayah*, (fem), from *reya'* meaning friend or female friend].[12]

Jesus said in John 15:14, "Ye are my *friends*, if ye do whatsoever I *command* you."

The Greek word translated as *command* is *entellomai*. It is a compound word including *en* ("inside core"), and *tellos* ("end, objective, goal"), plus *omai* (indicates the middle voice).

Taken together, this word means that Jesus "puts within His developing Bride the objective and goal which He desires her to become."

This is, indeed, a command; but not a harsh command from a drill sergeant in the army. It is instead a loving, caring invitation (even a challenge) to become our very best self in response to His offer of deeper fellowship with Himself.

In John 15, Jesus described an historical change in His relationship with His followers, one that changed everything for His disciples and those who believed after them.

CHAPTER 1 – FRIEND

*Henceforth I call you not servants; for the servant knoweth not what his lord doeth: but I have called you **friends**; for all things that I have heard of my Father I have made known unto you.*
(John 15:15, emphasis mine)

This unique relationship was foreshadowed in other places within the Old Testament as well. God expressed it through the prophet Isaiah when He said:

"*But thou, Israel, art my servant, Jacob whom I have chosen, the seed of Abraham my **friend**.*" (Isaiah 41:8, emphasis mine)

The Hebrew word translated "friend" in this passage is *ahab*, which means "to love, like, have affection for ..."

As a Friend of the Bridegroom, we have simply taken the *first step* in our first stage of relationship with Jesus. There are two more steps in this first stage marked by "Hunger" for Him.

The Bridegroom calls His "purchased one" *three* progressive names in the earliest chapters of the Song:

1. **Friend** (love companion)

2. **Fairest Among Women** or "most beautiful of women" from Song of Solomon 1:8. At this early stage, the Bridegroom calls her "fairest among women" because of the Holy Spirit in her, but she is not yet His "bride."

3. **Dove**, which appears in Song of Solomon 2:14.

From the second step forward, we begin to understand that He knows us, and calls us by name to follow Him onward.

THE MAKING OF A BRIDE

Endnotes

1. J. Hudson Taylor, M.R.C.S., *Union and Communion or Thoughts on the Song of Solomon*, Third Ed. (London: Morgan & Scott, 12 Paternoster Buildings, e.c.; China Inland Missions, Newington Green, 1914). NOTE: This book is in the public domain, and is available in E-book form from numerous trustworthy Internet sources.

2. Drawn from comments written by J. Stuart Holden, in his Foreword to the 1914 edition of *Union and Communion*.

3. Many modern translations favor the translations "cliff" or "steep place." The Hebrew word translated as "stair" in the phrase, "secret places of the stair," is *madregah*.

4. *Gesenius' Lexicon* says *madrega(h)* (translated as "stairs" in Song 2:14) means *"a steep mountain,* which one had to ascend *by steps,* as though it were *a ladder.* (Also appears in Ezek. 38:20.) Blue Letter Bible. 1996-2012. 10 Sep 2012. < http:// www.blueletterbible.org/lang/lexicon/lexicon.cfm? Strongs=H4095&t=KJV >.

5. *Strong's Exhaustive Concordance* says H4095, *madregah*, is "from an unused root meaning to *step.*" Blue Letter Bible. "Dictionary and Word Search for *madregah (Strong's 4095)."*

6. A.B. Simpson, *Loving as Jesus Loves: A Devotional Exposition of the Song of Song* (Camp Hill, PA: Christian Publications, 1996).

7. L.D. Johnson, *Proverbs, Ecclesiastes, Song of Solomon—Layman's Bible Book Commentary*, Vol. 9 (Nashville: Broadman Press, 1982).

8. Ibid.

9. J.H. Taylor, *Union and Communion*, p. 2.

10. This numerological portrait emerges when one multiplies the 12 Old Testament Patriarchs times the 12 New Testament Apostles to equal 144—then this number is multiplied by 1,000, which often portrays eternity in biblical numerology.

11. If you are unfamiliar with the term "woo," it means "to seek the favor, affection, or love of another, especially in the context of marriage."

12. Strong's H7474.

Chapter 2

STAIRSTEP 2
GOD PURSUER

HUNGRY FOR MORE ...

"Let him kiss me with the kisses of his mouth: for thy love is better than wine.

"Because of the savour of thy good ointments thy name is as ointment poured forth, therefore do the virgins love thee.

"Draw me, we will run after thee...*we will be glad and rejoice in thee, we will remember thy love more than wine ..."*
(Song of Solomon 1:2-4, emphasis mine)

In the early part of the Song of Solomon, the Bride speaks much ... *way too much!* Later, however, as she matures she speaks little *and* listens more.

This is the influence of *hunger* on the human soul. This is the best kind of hunger, the hunger that births *the soul's cry after God!*

LET HIM KISS ME ...

When the Shulamite woman says, *"Let him kiss me with the kisses of his mouth,"* the deep meanings of the key Hebrew words in this passage are virtually lost in translation! They fail to make the transition into the English language without some serious help.

The Hebrew word translated as "kiss" comes from the Hebrew root *nashaq*.[1] It means "to equip with weapons"!

The noun or "name" form, *nesheq*, is translated "kisses." It means *"arsenal, armor."* The word translated "mouth" (*peh*), produces another surprising meaning: "word, speech."

Rephrased with these deeper meanings from the original Hebrew, we now hear the Shulamite cry out:

*"Let him **equip me with weapons** with the **arsenal and armor of His Word**."*

Surprised? This is just the beginning of the hidden treasure awaiting us in this powerful book of the Bible!

As new Christians, we soon sense a hunger that births *our soul's cry after God.* Our soul is already purchased and we have found peace through the blood of the Lamb on the Cross.

We are already saved and enjoying "new life in Christ" at this point. We know we are "heaven-bound" and we have the proverbial "fire insurance" of salvation through grace. Some at this point may even ask, "That's great! Isn't that all there is?"

In Solomon's Song, we really don't know how long the Shulamite has been his friend. Perhaps she has been on "pause" at the "friend" stage of her relationship with him for many years.

How many Christians have stalled in their spiritual journey to "camp around the salvation fire" when there is so much more awaiting them as they follow Jesus while bearing their cross?[2]

THIS IS ONE OF THE GREAT TRAGEDIES
OF CHRISTIAN LIFE:
ETERNAL SECURITY WITH
NO INTERNAL STRENGTH
OR EVERLASTING SIGNIFICANCE.

CHAPTER 2 - GOD-CHASER

Our relationship with Jesus Christ is meant to take us upward "from glory to glory," not bog down our progress in some static and increasingly lifeless and fruitless holding pattern.[3]

Vision had come into the life of the Shulamite woman and she would never again be content *in His absence!* The same thing happens in our lives with Christ.

DO YOU REMEMBER THE DAY?

Do you remember the day when hunger for Him arrived, and you knew *the world* would never fully satisfy you again?

The Shulamite found her heart "strangely moved" as never before, and she instinctively cried out for *more!*

> DO YOU REMEMBER WHEN YOU FIRST BECAME HUNGRY FOR HIM?

(This was how a discouraged Oxford-educated Anglican priest named John Wesley described his encounter with God. It happened when he reluctantly attended a Moravian meeting in London and felt his heart "strangely moved" by the Spirit. After this intimate experience with God, Wesley began a spiritual journey with Jesus that helped launch the Great Awakening throughout Europe and the American colonies!)

Job understood discouragement. He was no stranger to the sorrow of separation from God, or to crushing grief in this life. Yet, he refused to raise his voice and curse God. Instead he cried out, *"Oh that I knew where I might find Him ..."* (Job 23:3a).

The moment of illumination and desire in the human heart is so precious to the Lord that He immortalized it in the fourth Beatitude when He said:

> *"Blessed are they **which do hunger** and thirst after righteousness: for they shall be filled."*
> (Matthew 5:6, emphasis mine)

LET HIM KISS ME

By the power of the Holy Spirit working within us, we cry out for more with the heart and longing of the Shulamite for her Beloved, "Let Him *kiss* me ..."

The Shulamite wasn't asking for a kiss of reconciliation like the Father's kiss for his prodigal son in Jesus' parable (as wonderful as that is).

> *"And [the Prodigal son] arose, and came to his father. But when he was yet a great way off, his father saw him, and had compassion, and ran, and fell on his neck, and **kissed him**."*
> (Luke 15:20, insertion and emphasis mine)

This kiss of joyful reunion is wonderful. Luke uses the Greek word, *kataphileo*, which means "to kiss earnestly with intense love." One scholar says it means "to kiss much, kiss again and again, kiss tenderly."[4]

In the Shulamite's cry, we see there is *much more* than this wonderful picture of reconciling love between a prodigal son and a loving father!

The Holy Spirit working within the Shulamite's heart moves her to cry out for more! She is crying out for the *Son's* kiss of intimacy, communion, and affection.

This kiss is different from the Father's kiss of reconciliation and reunion in some very important ways. This is a plea for intimate closeness—a quality we only find through *relationship*.

CHAPTER 2 - GOD-CHASER

This new step or stage in the Shulamite's journey with Solomon is marked by something remarkable: *She wants **him**, not just "**his**."* (She didn't come to this new level totally on her own—God Himself draws out this longing for relationship in the human heart.)

The apostle Paul wrote in the Book of Romans:

"For whom He did foreknow, He also did predestinate (to be) conformed to the image of His Son." (Romans 8:29a)

Jesus said:

*"No man can come to Me, except the Father which hath sent Me **draw him** ..."* (John 6:44a, italics mine).

This lands us squarely in the theological battle zone between the Calvinists and Armenians. This is an incredibly complex area with lengthy biblical arguments on both sides; nevertheless I offer this brief summary because we see God's insight about this controversy in The Song of Solomon:

Calvinists believe God predestines all who will accept Christ, and that the final equation of who gets saved and who is damned is settled totally through divine sovereignty regardless of human choices.

The *Armenian* view sees salvation or damnation as the product of choices we make through our free will, but it is *also understood* that the Holy Spirit prepares the way through grace for us to hear and receive Christ.

I confess that I am a *"Cal-menian,"* because I find true Bible principles and a few extreme positions on both sides. I choose to take what seems true from both and discard or minimize any less valid or less important points.

THE MAKING OF A BRIDE

In Jesus, God can and does embrace His own sovereignty *and* His own freedom in His dealings with us! Let me say it in a way worthy of display on your refrigerator:

"The Soul must always have a heavenly vision to draw it out of itself, and away from the things of earth."

J. Hudson Taylor penned this poem describing the heavenly blend of Divine provision with human decision in the journey of life:

In the secret of His presence,
How my soul delights to hide!
Oh, how precious are the lessons
Which I learn at Jesus' side!

Earthly cares can never vex me.
Neither trials lay me low;
For when Satan comes to vex me,
To the secret place I go!

THE SOUL'S VISION

The Shulamite continues with one of the most quoted sentences in the Bible: *"Thy love is better than wine"* (Song of Solomon 1:2a).

Now her eyes are opened to see the grand scale of love awaiting her. It outmatches the intoxication produced by any earthly product of fermentation.

The Hebrew word for "love" in this passage, *dod*, is always used in the *plural* form as *loves*. Hudson Taylor noted that it often speaks of "endearments and caresses." The use of "wine" speaks of *joy, fullness,* and *plenty.*

CHAPTER 2 - GOD-CHASER

We show ourselves unworthy of the wooing of the Bridegroom if we continue to *think of what we have "given up."*

— Jessie Penn-Lewis

I will gladly drop the appetizer the moment the main course arrives! After all, Solomon is describing *experiences of God's Presence!*

He is saying, "These experiences of Thy Manifest Presence—these are better than wine! These blessed times are *better* than *all* that they cost." This tells us that once we have this "high" we will never be fully satisfied *without His Presence.*

We quickly learn that we lose only the *dross* when we exchange earthly "treasures" for heavenly ones (found only in His Presence).

I was hell-bound and happy to tag along for the ride before God finally broke through and I received Jesus as my Lord and Savior.

Once I was in His Kingdom, however, I refocused my life on God's priorities and led my parents and large family to Jesus within six months. The Lord helped me move rapidly from "spiritual virgin" to "reproducing bride" in Christ! I was not yet a "bride" at the stage when this occurred.

All that is of the earth is temporary; God satisfies forever.

*"Jesus answered and said unto her, Whosoever drinketh of this water **shall** thirst again:*

*"But whosoever drinketh of the water that I shall give him shall **never** thirst; but the water that I shall give him shall be in him a well of water springing up into everlasting life."*

(John 4:13-14, emphasis mine)

THE MAKING OF A BRIDE

Jesus freely offers each of us the Water of Life, but it always comes down to this simple truth: *the soul must choose.*

THE SOUL'S CHOICE

> *"...thy **name** is as **ointment** poured forth, therefore do the virgins love thee.*
>
> **"Draw me, we will run after thee ..."**
>
> (Song of Solomon 1:3b-4a, emphasis mine)

The Hebrew word translated as "ointment" is *shemen*. It means "olive oil with many uses, or *anointing from within* for many uses." The root word, *shem*, means "character" or one's "inner self." Therefore, *shemen,* or ointment, also speaks of "character" or one's "inner self"; which is "portable."

Ironically, the literal Latin word for "seed" is *semen*. Its use in the English language perfectly expresses this capacity of holy *ointment* or *anointing oil* to contain and pass on the imprint of God's "character" or "inner self" to humanity.

The *Name* represents the Person of the Lord Jesus, which always attracts the Soul. You see, *our hearts need a Person!* (Mere "objects" never fully satisfy; only another *Subject* can do that.)

At this point, the Shulamite learns more about the Bridegroom's *character and nature.* She describes the process with a unique choice of words:

> *"Thy name is as ointment poured forth."* (Song of Solomon 1:3b)

This speaks of the Lord's inner character and nature being "poured out" upon waiting hearts. As *we* receive His very nature embedded in His name, we become "spiritually impregnated" and transformed with *His* virtue and nature.

CHAPTER 2 - GOD-CHASER

The Name of Jesus also carries with it at least three distinct forms of *anointing* "poured out" from the abundance within Him:

The Name of Jesus is an "ointment of healing."

God revealed that *healing* is one of His holy names in Exodus 15:26 when He declared, "I am the Lord that *healeth* thee" [or "I Am Jehovah Rapha"].

When the Lord Jesus launched His earthly ministry, He declared that His divine assignment included the anointing to heal earthly diseases and infirmities, and to bring wholeness to the afflicted as He quoted from Isaiah 61:

> *"The Spirit of the Lord is upon Me, because He hath anointed Me to preach the gospel to the poor; He hath sent Me to* **heal** *the brokenhearted, to preach deliverance to the captives, and recovering of sight to the blind, to set at liberty them that are bruised,*
>
> *"To preach the acceptable year of the Lord."*
>
> (Luke 4:18, emphasis mine)

The Name of the Lord is an "ointment of anointing."

The Lord's heavenly seal of approval came from the words in Isaiah's prophecy that declared: "The Spirit of the Lord God is upon me, *because the Lord hath* **anointed Me** ..." (Isaiah 61:1a, emphasis mine).

> THE ANOINTING IS GOD'S SEAL OF APPROVAL.

The apostle Paul told the Corinthian believers, "Now He which stablisheth us with you in Christ, and *hath anointed us*, is God" (2 Corinthians 1:21, emphasis mine).

The Name of the Lord is an "ointment of comfort."

THE MAKING OF A BRIDE

God's gift of comfort saturates the Bible from cover to cover, because comfort is part of His nature and therefore, incorporated in the meaning and anointing inherent in His name:

> "Yea, though I walk through the valley of the shadow of death, I will fear no evil: for thou art with me; thy rod and thy staff they **comfort** me." (Psalm 23:4, emphasis mine)

> "The Spirit of the Lord God is upon Me; because the Lord hath anointed Me to preach good tidings unto the meek; He hath sent me to bind up the brokenhearted, to proclaim liberty to the captives, and the opening of the prison to them that are bound;

> "To proclaim the acceptable year of the Lord, and the day of vengeance of our God; to **comfort** all that mourn;

> "To appoint unto them that mourn in Zion, to give unto them beauty for ashes, the oil of joy for mourning, the garment of praise for the spirit of heaviness; that they might be called trees of righteousness, the planting of the Lord, that He might be glorified." (Isaiah 61:1-3, emphasis mine)

> "And I will pray the Father, and He shall give you another **Comforter**, that He [the Holy Spirit] may abide with you forever." (John 14:16, emphasis mine)

The "third person" in the Song of Solomon isn't a person at all—it is the collective group of young virgins around the Shulamite woman:

> **"Therefore do the 'hidden ones' love Thee ..."**
> (Song of Solomon 1:3b)

The Hebrew term translated as "hidden ones" in this verse is *almah*, which means *"virgins, young marriageable women."*[5]

(The New Testament Greek equivalent to *almah* is *parthenos*. It is the root word for Parthenon, the name of perhaps the most

CHAPTER 2 - GOD-CHASER

famous Greek temple ruin in Athens. "The Parthenon" is a temple originally built to house a gold and ivory statue of Athena, held by ancient Athenians to be their patron goddess of wisdom.)

The picture of spiritual virgins in the Song of Solomon clearly describes **"those in God's Kingdom who are saved but not yet the Bride"** (you can't be a bride *and* a virgin). *It represents those who are saved and hungry for Him—but not yet intimate with Him, or reproductive of His character and gracious works.*

The apostle Paul tried to convey his own hunger to *know* the Lord Jesus more intimately to the Philippian believers:

"I count all things but loss for the excellency of the knowledge of Christ Jesus my Lord: for whom I have suffered the loss of all things, and do count them but dung, that I may win Christ,

"And be found in him, not having mine own righteousness, which is of the law, but that which is through the faith of Christ, the righteousness which is of God by faith:

"That I may know him, *and the power of his resurrection, and the fellowship of his sufferings, being made conformable unto his death;*

"If by any means I might attain unto the resurrection of the dead."   (Philippians 3:8b-11, emphasis mine)

Paul uses the Greek term *ginōskō*, when he says "that I may *know* Him ..." It means to learn to know, come to know, get knowledge of, perceive, or feel.[6] This term is nearly as powerful as the Hebrew equivalent, *yada*, which essentially means "to become one with...."

Paul is talking about *knowing* the Lord experientially, as opposed to intuitively (as would be implied through the Greek word, *eido*). As believers and "God-pursuers," we should long to understand, experience, feel, be conscious of, and radiate the nature and presence of Jesus Christ.

The Shulamite woman then says:

> *"Draw me, we will run after thee ... we will be glad and rejoice in thee, we will remember thy love more than wine ..."*
> (Song of Solomon 1:4, emphases mine)

This heart-hunger for HIM *is the key!* Hunger for Him separates the Bride from the virgins! God gives this hunger to *everyone* who is converted, but *not all act on it!* This is why there are "spiritual virgins" on every single stage of this journey *until* the final stage when the Groom takes the Bride to bed.

As the purchased one follows on to know Him, these *virgins* will be drawn too.

If we do not move forward, we hinder others! The Shulamite cries out in "intercessory prayer" on behalf of the virgins around her as well as herself when she says, "Draw me, and *we* will run after thee ..."

"DRAW ME, AND WE WILL RUN AFTER THEE ..."

The Song continues, "*We* will be glad and rejoice in thee, *we* will remember thy love more than wine...."

King Solomon was quoting key words from his father's "wedding song" in Psalm 45, a song that also illustrates the relationship of the virgins to the King's Bride:

> *"She shall be brought unto the king in raiment of needlework:* **the virgins her companions** *that follow her shall be brought unto thee.*
>
> *"With gladness and rejoicing shall they be brought:* they *shall enter into the king's palace."*
> (Psalm 45:14-15, emphasis mine)

CHAPTER 2 - GOD-CHASER

The work of the drawing is His—we respond as He draws; we abandon ourselves to His leadership into intimacy.

Consider two witnesses who confirm this divine operation in the wooing process, one from the Old Covenant and one from the New:

> *"The Lord hath appeared of old unto me, saying, Yea, I have loved thee with an everlasting love: therefore with lovingkindness have* **I drawn thee***."*
> (Jeremiah 31:3, emphasis mine)

> *"No man can come to me, except the Father which hath sent me* **draw him***: and I will raise him up at the last day."*
> (John 6:44, emphasis mine)

As with every work of God in our lives, there is divine purpose in the process; and a destination where we encounter more transformation into the likeness of Christ. Our next destination speaks of intimacy in the King's Chambers.

THE MAKING OF A BRIDE

End Notes

1. NOTE: A *transliterated* Greek, Hebrew, or Aramaic word is reproduced in our English language using English letters to approximate the *sound* of the word in its original language.

2. See this in all three Synoptic Gospels—Matthew 16:24, Mark 8:34, Luke 9:23.

3. See 2 Corinthians 3:18.

4. "Dictionary and Word Search for *kataphileō (Strong's G2705),*" *Blue Letter Bible*. 1996-2012. 28 Sep 2012. < http:// www.blueletterbible.org/lang/lexicon/lexicon.cfm? Strongs=G2705&t=KJV >.

5. Ibid, *`almah (Strong's H5959).*

6. Ibid, *ginōskō (Strong's G1097).*

CHAPTER 3

STAIRSTEP 3
LOVER

EXPERIENCES OF INTIMACY

*"Draw me, we will run after Thee: The King hath **brought me into his chambers**: we will be glad and rejoice in Thee. We will **make mention of** [KJV—remember] thy love… [in uprightness] do they love Thee."*
(Song of Solomon 1:4, emphasis mine)

The word translated as "make mention of" or "remember" is the Hebrew word, **zakhar**. It simply means *"to focus upon."*

You find there is much more power in this word when you dig deeper. (This is probably the only way to grasp the meaning Solomon wanted to express in this passage!)

Spiros Zodhiates, in *The Complete Word Study Dictionary,* said *zakhar* has "three sets of meanings with overlapping mental states and external actions":[1]

1. To remember, recollect, reflect upon
2. To mention, declare, proclaim
3. To record, commemorate [praise]

In other words, this one word moves us powerfully from *fleeting memory* to *permanent praise!*[2]

THE MAKING OF A BRIDE

Choose Him, and He will draw you into His inner chambers.

As soon as the Shulamite woman chose Him alone, she proclaimed, "[In uprightness] do they love Thee" (Song of Solomon 1:4).

This tells us *our divine Bridegroom wants intimacy with us as much or more than we want intimacy with Him!* He wants to draw us more than we want to be drawn by Him.

This is *more* than an invitation to the "banqueting table"—it is *an invitation to the King's inner chambers* for *intimacy.*

He wants each of us to know Him more fully. Notice that the public banquet always follows *after* the private chambers. First He gently draws us into intimacy in His chambers—*then* come His gifts.

The richest gifts of God come in intimate union with Him. He gives us the free gift of eternal life—and then invites us to receive *Him!* Once we embrace Him, then we can receive His many spiritual gifts.

The words of an old song chorus, "Shut In With God," beautifully express the special nature of our personal invitation to enter into the Lord's inner chambers:

"Shut in with God in the secret place,
There, in the spirit, beholding His face.
Finding more power to run in the race,
Oh I long to be shut in with God."[3]

The Beloved has already given her the gift of **eternal life**; *now He can give her the gift of* **Himself**. Eternal life comes at conversion.

CHAPTER 3 – LOVER

The priceless gift of "Himself" comes in intimacy, worship, and Bridehood.

Now her focus begins to move from **her consecration** *to Him to* **His indwelling, inward-working Person within her.**

These two levels of intimacy actually picture the two different dimensions of relationship common in most churches.

The first level is occupied by the largest group, composed of perhaps 95% of all believers in Jesus Christ. The people in this majority group focus on *their consecration* and *good works* done for the Lord.

The remaining 5% of the believers who comprise the second level tend to focus on *His* in-dwelling, in-working Person within them.

*"The King hath brought me in ... **We will be glad** ... will [zakhar] make mention of [focus upon] Thy love [!] ..."*

(Song of Solomon 1:4, emphasis mine)

FOLLOWING CHRIST IS NOT ABOUT YOU, BUT HIM.

The Shulamite is learning to focus upon the Beloved and celebrate Him as her chief joy and delight. As long as your emphasis is upon what *you* do for Him, then your Christian life and service is "all about you." Remember, following Christ is not about you, but Him.

When you speak less and let Him talk to you and speak His truth about you, then you will hear Him reveal the wonderful things He has deposited in you. Then you can actually watch those things He declares about you come to pass!

THE MAKING OF A BRIDE

The Shulamite woman is learning to rejoice in *Him*, not merely in His gifts, or in her own consecration or works done *for* Him. His gifts to you, and your good works done for Him, are important and have their proper place in your life. However, they must never take *first* place in your affections or worship—that is reserved solely for the Beloved Himself.

> "***Delight*** *thyself also in the Lord: and He shall give thee the desires of thine heart."*   *(Psalm 37:4, emphasis mine)*

The word translated as "delight" in this psalm is *anag*, a Hebrew word with three possible meanings:

1. "To become pliable" (like a yielded bride in the arms of her husband).

2. "To be effeminate."

3. "To be sporting but aggressive."

There are many layers of potentially confusing and complex word meanings such as this in the Song of Solomon, purposely written that way in my opinion for maximum impact upon his readers at that time. (This may explain why so many cannot handle this book of the Bible!)

With the three additional insights into the original Hebrew word for "delight" in this passage, it takes on the expanded meaning, "to be happy about, to take *exquisite delight in*" the Lord.[4]

We are called to *focus on and track God*. I really like the title of the book by Tommy Tenney entitled, *The God Chasers*.[5] I believe we are all anointed and appointed to become God chasers or pursuers.

CHAPTER 3 – LOVER

In his second book, *The God Catchers*, Tenney captures the wonder in the Shulamite's words in Song of Solomon 1:4 quoted earlier:

"In some supernatural way, *the pursuer becomes the pursued* when God catches wind of our worship and praise."[6]

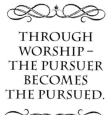

THROUGH WORSHIP – THE PURSUER BECOMES THE PURSUED.

As the Shulamite woman learned to pull her focus away from merely good things to concentrate on the Beloved, she received His invitation to come closer in the inner chamber.

Keep in mind that this kind of focus on the Beloved is only possible for one with "a clear conscience void of offense toward God and men." (Acts 24:16)

"Let us draw near with a true heart in full assurance of faith, having our hearts sprinkled from an evil conscience, and our bodies washed with pure water." (Hebrews 10:22)

At this place in her journey, the Shulamite woman receives revelations that can come only during times of intimacy!

A TWO-FOLD REVELATION OF THE KING'S CHAMBERS

*"I am **black**, but **comely**, O ye daughters of Jerusalem, as the tents of Kedar, as the curtains of Solomon."*
(Song of Solomon 1:5, emphasis mine)

The Hebrew root translated "black" in this passage, *shachar*, doesn't mean black "as opposed to white." There is no gender, race, or color here or anywhere else in this book.

THE MAKING OF A BRIDE

(Remember Paul's statement in Galatians 3:28, NASB: "There is neither Jew nor Greek, there is neither slave nor free man, there is neither male nor female; for you are all one in Christ Jesus.")

Shachar in this passage means "dim, not translucent." Translucent is a compound word, or two words joined together. *Lucent* means light, and *trans* means "through." In other words, the light won't shine through her clearly. It means "not transparent."

The Shulamite accurately sees herself as impure, unclean, and not right. She knows she is not perfect and understands there is something inside that won't let His light shine all the way through.

Her Beloved sees this too, but calls her to come close in the King's Chambers to correct that problem for her.

We find *two revelations* within His Chambers in His "Manifested Presence."

#1: HIS MANIFESTED PRESENCE

*"And the likeness of the firmament upon the heads of the living creature was as the colour of the terrible **crystal**, stretched forth over their heads above."* (Ezekiel 1:22, emphasis mine)

The Hebrew word translated as "crystal" in this prophetic passage literally refers to frost or more specifically, *ice*, because of its similarity to crystal. Ice can possess many of the same qualities of a crystal—it can be:

1. *Opaque*, meaning it blocks or absorbs light and does not allow light to pass through it.

2. *Translucent* (or cloudy in appearance, allowing light to come through but does not allow any image to shine through).

CHAPTER 3 – LOVER

3. *Transparent*, allowing light to come through its structure unchanged, clearly displaying the original image of the light source to come through unchanged or unmodified. One of the odd abilities of crystals (including ice crystals) is the ability to actually amplify and enlarge an image that flows through it (think of a diamond).

Revelation 4:6 says, "And before the throne there was a sea of glass *like unto crystal*: and in the midst of the throne, and round about the throne, were four beasts full of eyes before and behind" (emphasis mine).

Again, John says in Revelation 22:1, "And He shewed me a pure river of water of life, *clear as crystal*, proceeding out of the throne of God and of the Lamb" (emphasis mine).

#2: HIS LIGHT REVEALS OUR "BLACKNESS"

Once we enter the intimate atmosphere of His chambers, we acquire *the same insight Job received* after his encounter with God at the end of his trial:

> "I have heard of thee by the hearing of the ear: but now mine eye seeth thee. Wherefore I abhor myself, and repent in dust and ashes." (Job 42:5-6)

Like Job before us, we see how much we are *not* like Him!

However, when the Shulamite woman refers to "my *blackness*," we should not interpret it as a reference to *the blackness of un-repented sins*.

Why not? These sins are dealt with at conversion! This refers to something much *deeper*, something that is an innate part of her humanity (and of ours).

THE MAKING OF A BRIDE

This pursuer of the Beloved began to feel *within herself* some "blackness" that stemmed directly from her creature-life, the fallen nature inherited from our fallen common ancestor, the First Adam.

The power of this fallen nature was broken and cleansed from the *God-ward side* in conversion. Now she must become *"in experience"* who she is by justification. This only comes *in union* with Him.

Here are three examples of transformations triggered by intimate exposure to the glory and holiness of God (including the reference to Job quoted earlier):

> *"Therefore I was left alone, and saw this great vision, and there remained no strength in me: for* **my comeliness was turned in me into corruption,** *and I retained no strength."*
> *(Daniel 10:8, emphasis mine)*

> *"I have heard of thee by the hearing of the ear: but now mine eye seeth thee. Wherefore* **I abhor myself,** *and repent in dust and ashes."* *(Job 42:5-6, emphasis mine)*

> *"In the year that King Uzziah died I saw also the Lord sitting upon a throne, high and lifted up, and His train filled the temple…*
>
> *"Then said I, Woe is me! for* **I am undone;** *because I am a man of unclean lips, and I dwell in the midst of a people of unclean lips: for* **mine eyes have seen the King,** *the Lord of hosts"*
> *(Isaiah 6:1, 5; emphasis mine)*

- *Daniel* has just completed his third week of fasting for his captive nation when the pre-incarnate Christ (sometimes called "the Angel of the Lord" in the Old Testament) visited him in answer to prayers he had prayed 21 days earlier.

CHAPTER 3 – LOVER

- *Job* had suffered the loss of virtually everything that mattered to him, and was beginning to waver when God spoke directly to him and revealed His glory to the dejected man sitting on a pile of ashes.

- *Isaiah* the prophet had mourned the death of King Uzziah for most of a year when the pre-incarnate Christ suddenly visited him in the temple. Isaiah's ministry underwent a radical change from that point forward to his martyrdom.

All three of these biblical leaders lived lives consecrated to God, despite great trials, sorrow, pain, and opposition. Yet, each of these men was "undone" and humbled by intimate revelations of the holiness and majesty of God in His glory.

**When the self-abhorrence is real and deep,
the Soul *does not try to hide it*.**

"Blind Bartimaeus" underscores this truth in the Gospel of Mark:

"And they came to Jericho: and as He went out of Jericho with His disciples and a great number of people, blind Bartimaeus, the son of Timaeus, sat by the highway side begging.

"And when He heard that it was Jesus of Nazareth, he began to cry out, and say, Jesus, thou son of David, have mercy on me.

"And many charged him that he should hold his peace: **but he cried the more a great deal, Thou son of David, have mercy on me.**

"And Jesus stood still, and commanded him to be called. And they call the blind man, saying unto him, Be of good comfort, rise; He calleth thee.

THE MAKING OF A BRIDE

"And he, casting away his garment, rose, and came to Jesus.

"And Jesus answered and said unto him, What wilt thou that I should do unto thee? The blind man said unto Him, Lord, that I might receive my sight.

"And Jesus said unto him, Go thy way; thy faith hath made thee whole. And immediately he received his sight, and followed Jesus in the way."
(Mark 10:46-52, emphasis mine)

Blind Bartimaeus "Cried all the more, 'Jesus, have mercy!'" the closer Jesus came. This is a lesson in "the ascendency of God." In other words, it helps us realize that God is God, and we *are not*. He is "the Rock who is higher than I" (see Psalm 16:2).

Many want their carnal nature dealt with
***in private*, often due to *pride*.**

Wise people are quick to "humble themselves under the hand of almighty God, that He may exalt them in due time."[7]

Pride *must be broken* for deliverance to come. Bartimaeus threw away his pride along with his cloak that day.

He was already at the bottom rung of the social ladder because of his status as a blind beggar. Yet, the act of crying out and casting off the cloak drew uncomfortable public attention and ridicule that would normally be avoided.

When the cloak fell, so did his identity, any "rights" he may have had, and any sense of "place" he possessed.

> APPEARANCE MUST BE SURRENDERED FOR TRANSPARENCY.

"Appearance" must be surrendered for *transparency*. The crowd demanded that the beggar go back to the monotonous roadside begging they were accustomed to from him. However, the nearer Jesus came, the louder

CHAPTER 3 – LOVER

Bartimaeus cried out! He was determined to bare his soul in transparency to the only One who could answer his heart's cry.

Transparent hunger for more of God often triggers jealousy, resentment, and misunderstanding among those nearby who are content with their status quo.

"I am *black*, but comely, O ye daughters."

This is a "spiritual virgin" speaking to other believers in the church—believers who may be tempted to criticize anyone who willingly embraces change. They don't want anyone to "rock the boat" when they are clinging desperately to the perceived safety of their relatively dry and lifeless religious routine.

*"I am black in myself as the rough **tents** of Kedar."*

The Shulamite woman says her lack of transparency is like or similar to the Hebrew word, *ohel*. It is defined as "nomad's tent (speaking of transience), hut, home."[8] It speaks of a person's *outward* or visible traits.

I'm referring more to the *soul* than the body—the mind, will, and emotions. The "carnal" or fleshly nature operates and manipulates us through *the soul*.

Paul the apostle said, "For we know that the law is spiritual: but I am *carnal*, sold under sin" (Romans 7:14, emphasis mine).

He also said, "For ye are yet *carnal*: for whereas there is among you envying, and strife, and divisions, are ye not *carnal*, and walk as men?" (1 Corinthians 3:3, emphasis mine).

In the next breath, or in the second half of the passage in Song of Solomon 1:5, the Shulamite radically shifts her perspective:

*"But I am **beautiful** as the curtains of Solomon."*

THE MAKING OF A BRIDE

The Hebrew word for beautiful is *naveh*. It speaks of the *inside*, of the inward life of the human spirit in communion with God's Holy Spirit.

This young woman is receiving and describing a great revelation about the *reality* of the way her Beloved sees her (and the way He sees *us*). It illustrates the miraculous intervention of God to seek and to save us—the lost!

God didn't save us simply to throw us in a heavenly attic as static trophies soon to be forgotten. He has adopted us as His own children and *abides* or dwells with us for all of eternity![9]

In exchange, He desires our love, worship, and obedience.

THE SOUL'S KNOWLEDGE

*"If any man cometh unto me, and **hateth** not ... his own life ... he cannot be My disciple."*   (Luke 14:26, emphasis mine)

The word "hateth" in this passage comes from the Greek word, *iseo*. It means "to detest, to love less than something else." In this case, it means to love Jesus *so much more* that *in comparison*, your genuine love for your parents would almost seem to be the opposite of love.

"Look not upon me ... because the sun hath scorched me. My mother's sons were incensed against me; they made me keeper of the vineyards; but mine own vineyard have I not kept."
    (Song of Solomon 1:6)

The "purchased one" was *appointed by others* to be "keeper of the vineyards." The Beloved had nothing to do with assigning her to "busy-ness" in ministry.

Sadly, this accurately describes what happens in many believers in our churches—other people encourage them to "get busy *for* God" rather than to be "found *in Him.*"[10]

CHAPTER 3 – LOVER

"God will never give you work that takes away worship!"

She begins to understand the fruitlessness of "all work and no worship." It should be obvious that it is *not* bad to work for God. However, you can spiritually "dry up" if you "work" for God without worshiping God.

The Lord Jesus rebuked the church at Ephesus in Revelation 2:4 because the people had "lost their first love" for Him. (Notice that first He recognized their works, their labor, and their patience. The Lord praised them for laboring and not fainting, but warned that *He had something against them* because something far more important to Him was *missing!*)

The Shulamite had been "distracted about much serving" like Martha, the older sister of Mary and Lazarus in the Gospels; and failed to focus on her Lord (see Luke 10:40).

Jesus specifically corrected Martha for being "cumbered about" (KJV) in that situation. It comes from the Greek word, *perispao*, which means literally "to drag around in a circle."[11]

(Are you dragging your *ministry* around in a circle—or worse, is your ministry dragging *you* around in a circle and leading you to ignore Jesus in the process?)

This is why we say again, *"God will never give you work that takes away worship!"* We all need *time* to grow in relationship with God and with each other.

She also begins to feel the pain of being *misunderstood by others*. *"My mother's children* were angry with me…" (Song of Solomon 1:6b).

The Shulamite's siblings (many modern translations translate this as "My mother's sons") became angry at her self-reproach because *her honesty also illuminated the depth of their unrecognized and unrepentant sin.* The "mother's children" pictured here also represent "the church" or general body of believers who tend to keep up just enough to get by and be included.

The Shulamite was "living a good life, working for God; and being used of God" so to speak. But it wasn't enough.

She longed for more and was willing to do whatever was necessary to pursue more; but the virgins and her brothers were thinking, "What more *is* there?"

They asked, "What's the problem? Don't be negative—do you think you're better than the rest of us?"

They were jealous—perhaps in the same way that Cain became jealous of his brother, Abel, in Genesis 4.

*They do not see what is happening as the Lord draws her **deeper**.* Those "nominal Christians" never do. The Beloved was calling His Shulamite bride into balance, for **work without worship can cause burnout!**

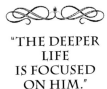

"THE DEEPER LIFE IS FOCUSED ON HIM."

-A.W. TOZER

They had allowed the "hunger key" to become frozen in the lock, so they never really opened the door to His *Presence* and *Person*.

A.W. Tozer said, "The deeper life is focused on *Him*." (At the same time, understand that you should never look at "the deeper life" as your life being spiritually "deeper" or better than another person's life.)

Never measure your spiritual life by comparing yourself or your ministry to others. Keep your eyes, your heart, and your ego or pride focused on Him. (Peter had this problem in John 21:20-22.

CHAPTER 3 – LOVER

Jesus dismissed his question about John's future status and said, "What is that to you? Follow thou Me.")

> *"Look not upon me...because the **sun** hath scorched me[!]"* (Song of Solomon 1:6a, emphasis mine)

The "sun" in this passage may well represent God Himself. Psalm 84:11 says, "The Lord God is a *Sun* and Shield..." (emphasis mine).

Isaiah the prophet experienced some "scorching" of his own when he personally encountered the King of glory:

> *"Then said I, Woe is me! for I am undone; because I am a man of unclean lips, and I dwell in the midst of a people of unclean lips: **for mine eyes have seen the King, the Lord of hosts.***
>
> *"Then flew one of the seraphims unto me, having a live coal in his hand, which he had taken with the tongs from off the altar:*
>
> *"And **he laid it upon my mouth**, and said, Lo, this hath touched thy lips; and thine iniquity is taken away, and thy sin purged."* (Isaiah 6:5-7, emphasis mine)

Daniel the prophet endured the indignity of captivity in the palaces of Babylon and Persia and persevered with legendary prayer and faith. Yet, he also discovered the shallow value of human strength and earthly virtue in the presence of God:

> *"Therefore I was left alone, and saw this great vision, and there remained **no strength** in me: for my comeliness was **turned in me into corruption**, and **I retained no strength**."*
> (Daniel 10:8, emphasis mine)

Job, the righteous man who endured Satan's brutal attempts to abort his love for God through unjust affliction, also knew what it was like to discover his earthly righteousness still wasn't worthy:

THE MAKING OF A BRIDE

> *"I have heard of thee by the hearing of the ear: but now mine eye seeth thee.*
>
> *"Wherefore **I abhor myself**, and repent in dust and ashes."*
> (Job 42:5-6, emphasis mine)

This may also symbolize the shallowness of all of the sacrificial work the Shulamite had done for her Beloved while laboring in the vineyards. Good works, selfless ministry, and sacrificial labor on behalf of others—but *without worship or true intimacy with the Beloved*—can *produce burnout.*

ENCOUNTERING THE "SUN OF RIGHTEOUSNESS" WITHOUT INTIMACY, LEADS TO BURNOUT.

Whenever one of us encounters God in the glory of intimacy or revelation, any works we have to offer Him suddenly look very inadequate if (and because) our worship and adoration are sadly lacking. Again, if you encounter the "Sun of Righteousness" without loving intimacy, you encounter *burnout* because anything we do on our own never measures up.

Elijah the prophet understood burnout. It hit him only a short time after personally orchestrating one of the Bible's most dramatic showdowns with demonic powers. Elijah singlehandedly faced, humiliated, and killed 450 prophets of Baal and scores of prophetesses of Ashtoreth in front of all of Israel.

When that mighty prophet heard that Queen Jezebel had vowed to kill him in revenge, the prophet's courage drained away and suddenly he began running for his life. He ended up alone, hungry and battling despair in the wilderness.

> *"But he himself went a day's journey into the wilderness, and came and sat down under a juniper tree: and **he requested***

CHAPTER 3 – LOVER

for himself that he might die; and said, It is enough; now, O Lord, take away my life; for I am not better than my fathers." (1 Kings 19:4, emphasis mine)

The Soul is very conscious of *herself*, her *feelings*, and her *appearance*. As for the Shulamite, her encounter with the Beloved in His inner chambers had triggered transformation. The **self-consciousness of her soul was giving way** to something far better. **All desire to be honored** or looked-up to **was passing away**.

This is the third of the initial three steps or stages I call *the self-conscious stages*:

First the bride-in-waiting gets saved.

Second, she develops spiritual hunger for her divine Bridegroom.

And *third*, she begins to *experience* Him. That is when her self-concerns begin to fade in importance and urgency.

This is progress! When you stop thinking about self and begin to think about Him, *transformation has begun*.

At this point, the "soul" is *transitioning* to the next stage of the journey and a whole new level of growth.

THE MAKING OF A BRIDE

End Notes

1. Spiros Zodhiates, *Complete Word Study Dictionary: New Testament* (Chattanooga, TN: AMG Publishers, 1992); *zakhar* (#H2142, verb).
2. Ibid, see *zecher* (#H2143, noun).
3. Author unknown, thought to be in the Public Domain.
4. Strong's, H6026.
5. Tommy Tenney, *The God Chasers* (Shippensburg, PA: Destiny Image Publishers, Inc., 1998).
6. Tommy Tenney, *The God Catchers* (Nashville, TN: Thomas Nelson, Inc., 2000), p. 4; italic emphasis mine.
7. See First Peter 5:6.
8. Strong's, H168.
9. See Romans 8:15, Galatians 4:6.
10. See Philippians 3:9, "And be found in him, not having mine own righteousness, which is of the law, but that which is through the faith of Christ, the righteousness which is of God by faith."
11. For additional information, see Strong's G4049.

STAGE B

RELATIONSHIPS

FROM TRANSPARENT RELATIONSHIP TO SURRENDER

The Fourth Stairstep – Fairest Among Women

Chapter 4 – Experiences to Relationship
Chapter 5 – The Well-Beloved's Instructions
Chapter 6 – The King's Table

The Fifth Stairstep – Communion With Him – Dove
Chapter 7 — Devoted

The Sixth Stairstep – Surrender to Him – Separated
Chapter 8 – Vulnerable

THE MAKING OF A BRIDE

Chapter 4

STAIRSTEP 4
FAIREST AMONG WOMEN

FROM EXPERIENCES TO RELATIONSHIP

"Tell me, O Thou whom my soul loveth, where Thou feedest Thy flock, where Thou makest it to rest at noon: for why should I be as one that [wandereth]?" (Song of Solomon 1:7)

As the Shulamite's soul cries to the Beloved, she reveals a deep desire to move from intermittent *experiences* to permanent *relationship* with the Bridegroom.

Her entire focus shifts from casual attraction to serious romance. She turns away from the misjudgments of others, feelings of unworthiness, and "busy work" for God. Instead, she *turns to Him.*

"He will understand," she is saying. It seems she has finally found someone who will genuinely love and understand her.

She has moved on from "being saved" to experiencing hunger and actually feeling miserable without Him!

Many Christians find satisfaction by merely attending meetings to get blessed, sing and dance, and find temporary happiness in God's presence in the church. Then they *go home* and call it good. And it is.

All of these things are good. Participate and sink your roots deep, but remember these *things* and activities are not *Him*. They are *His*.

Never *substitute* them for Him. That goes for all-night prayer meetings, cell groups, your work in the church, and even your evangelism efforts.

> WORKS WITHOUT WORSHIP ARE OF LITTLE VALUE TO THE SOUL.

"Works without worship" are of little value to God. When we become satisfied with these normally good things and stop short of seeking Him, they become *enemies* opposing God's desires for us.

How could this be?

The Lord's chief desire is union with His Bride. He wants our focus to be upon *Him*, not merely on His work, His blessings, or even His holiness.

The Beloved knows something else about the Shulamite: *He knows how she loathes herself now without Him.* Do you like yourself when you're as spiritually dry as yesterday's toast and God seems far away and out of reach?

David wrote in Psalm 23 that the Good Shepherd stops his sheep twice a day, at noon and at night. At noon He feeds them and makes them lie down in green pastures beside still waters to restore their souls.

The Shulamite wanted to be with her Beloved at *noon*. She was saying in essence:

> "Lord, I want to be with You. It isn't enough just to walk with You and the flock in church business, or participate in formal prayer meetings and evangelism projects. *I want to know **You**, not just '**yours**.'*"

CHAPTER 4 – EXPERIENCES TO RELATIONSHIP

Only one thing separates the Bride from the virgins: the Bride is *hungry*.

Some Christians get too busy and put on a "Plaster of Paris smile" – a brittle false face that allows them to pretend that everything is wonderful. Meanwhile they dry up inside and lose their hunger for God.

The difference between the Bride and the virgins is her incessant hunger for the Beloved. It just will not quit.

Listen, God will deal with you at whatever level *you* allow. If you limit your intimacy with Him to one Christmas or Easter service per year, or to one day in seven, then God loves you enough to take it, even though it is less than best.

(Seriously, treating God in any "part-time" manner is an insult to the One who created you and then redeemed you for love. What if your spouse approached your marriage with this attitude?)

When the Shulamite says, "I want to be with you at noon," it marks the beginning of a whole new dimension with Him.

The beginning of the new life is likened unto daybreak, and its maturity to *noontime*, free from all mists and *shadows*.

Theology professors and commentators, C. F. Keil and F. Delitzsch, said the original Hebrew translated as "noon" in this passage signifies two things linked in one phrase: *double light*.[1]

Why? Sunlight at sunset or sunrise always casts a shadow. However, the noonday sun casts no shadows (and produces or allows no darkness).

At this point, the Shulamite woman had nothing to hide from her Beloved. She came in complete openness with no shadows. Sadly, most Christians never come to *this* place.

> *"The path of the just is as the shining light that shineth more and more unto the perfect day."* (Proverbs 4:18)

The perfect day is high noon, the moment of perfection *when the sun is totally above you and there are no shadows anywhere.*

When doubts and distractions give way to intimacy, revelation is inevitable.

Job 11:17 says, *"Thy life shall arise above the noonday. Though there be darkness, it shall be as the morning."*

Moses and Joshua provide strong examples of this "before and after" transition and transformation.

Moses' name in Hebrew is *Masha*. It means "deliverer, liberator, taker-outer." He led the Israelites out of Egypt and to the border of the Promised Land.

As long as the people were in the *wilderness* (Joshua 5:12), they had passing *experiences* of God such as the pillar of cloud by day and the pillar of fire by night; plus *visitations* of God's glory in the tabernacle. They also experienced His *provision* with their daily allotment of *manna* (food that always putrefied overnight).

"Wilderness Christians" in our era never come into *relationship* with God. They become satisfied with temporary visitations and flirting experiences.

Immaturity chases down every "hot" revival and "feel-good" church meeting offering a spark of blessing or fire in it. It is driven to pursue every big preacher who comes to town, but avoids the *relationship* offered by the local church.

CHAPTER 4 – EXPERIENCES TO RELATIONSHIP

Wilderness Christians gather up blessings every day to "make it through." Mature Christians are more interested in *being* a blessing than in hunting blessings.

Joshua took over and finally led the Hebrew children across the Jordan River into the Land of Promise and they:

- moved *from experiences of God* to *relationship with God*
- went from visitations to belonging
- shifted from slave-hood to nationhood
- progressed from a daily handout of manna to sowing seed by faith in the Land of Promise—and reaping blessings according to God's promises.

In the framework of personal faith, they started working with God to determine their own future. Their *own choices* and *faith* determined their destiny and level of blessing and prosperity in God.

Do you see the difference?

The Shulamite discovers the difference between a brief experience and an on-going, growing relationship. She wants to come into Canaan. "There's more and I want more!"

It is the will of God that each newborn Soul be led past the shadows and into the full light of *God* Himself.

God doesn't want you to live in shadows without His fullness. *Yet, many linger in the morning mists and do not come into the rest at noon.*

Most folks chase blessings and *feelings* instead of relationship and *fullness*. God wants a Bride who hungers for more than just blessings and feelings. The Beloved is pleased when He hears:

"Tell me about the *noon-tide rest* ... I don't want to be as one that wandereth, tossed to and fro."

Experience-chasers put experiences on a pedestal where they don't belong. I absolutely love those moments of God's "manifest presence" in worship, prayer or praise. I really don't like the expression, "Oh, God *showed up* in our meeting."

God never "went" anywhere. He is always present. Paul said, *"For in Him we live, and move, and have our being ..."* (Acts 17:28a). God doesn't show up. You and I are the ones who show up. God isn't a Cosmic Vagabond hopping spiritual freight trains to His next "showing."

- Many people still come to church to *get* a blessing.
- We are the church, gathered to be equipped for greater relationship with Him and one another, and to *be* the blessing.

Revelation in intimacy produces a whole different paradigm of church!

One of our teachers in the international school I founded wrote a book entitled, *Stop Going to Church*. At first I said, "I'm not sure I like this." Then I noticed the sub-title printed in smaller type. It said, *"And start **being** the church."* I liked it so much that we published the book for him!

The Shulamite asked the Beloved for more and was transformed from passive follower to passionate pursuer. Then He opened His mouth and spoke directly to her for the first time.

CHAPTER 4 – EXPERIENCES TO RELATIONSHIP

End Note

1. C.F. Keil and F. Delitzsch, "Proverbs, Ecclesiastes, Song of Solomon." *Commentary on the Old Testament*, Vol. VI (Grand Rapids: William B. Eerdmans, n.d.), *zakhar or tsahar,* noon. These highly respected Protestant theology professors wrote this multi-volume commentary in German in the 19th century. It was translated into English over a period of 128 years by five scholars and is considered by many to be "the best conservative biblical commentary of the older Protestant scholarship," and thought by some to be unsurpassed even to this day.

THE MAKING OF A BRIDE

Chapter 5

STAIRSTEP 4 – CONTINUED
FAIREST AMONG WOMEN

THE WELL-BELOVED'S INSTRUCTIONS: HIS FIRST WORDS

> *"Tell me, O Thou whom my soul loveth, where Thou feedest Thy flock, where Thou makest it to rest at noon: for why should I be as one that [wandereth]?"* (Song of Solomon 1:7)

I don't know how much God can talk to wilderness saints, or if they are even capable of understanding Him.

However, I do know that **once we come for *Him* rather than for what is *His*, He opens His mouth.**

When the Beloved spoke to the Shulamite for the first time, He said:

> ***"If Thou know not,*** *O thou **fairest** among women, go thy way forth by the footsteps of the flock, and feed thy kids [the lambs] beside the shepherd's tents."*
> (Song of Solomon 1:8, parenthetic insertion and brackets mine)

Notice the Beloved's response to the Shulamite. He said:

> ***"If Thou know not..."***

This answer to the Shulamite's question indicates that she is at least partly **responsible** for her ignorance.

THE MAKING OF A BRIDE

Most of us spend too much time in the wilderness chasing blessings, provisions, and the glory. There is nothing wrong with any of these blessings of God, but there is *more:* The Blesser Himself.

Even as a 14-year-old new convert to Christ, I sensed there was a deeper dimension *beyond* merely chasing blessings. The bride is meant to live in this special place of repose, rest and confidence in God. This intimate place is virtually unknown to the virgins.

He put a draw on her ...

The Beloved *initiated* this new stage by speaking to the Shulamite's heart. He put a draw on her just as He described in Jeremiah 31:3:

*"Yea, I have loved thee with an everlasting love: therefore with lovingkindness have I **drawn** thee."*

WHEN THE BELOVED SPEAKS, YOU ARE RESPONSIBLE TO RESPOND.

The Beloved's first words triggered a hunger to follow Him deeper into relationship. From that point forward, *she was responsible to respond.*

Your Beloved Savior has placed a draw on you as well. Don't expect Him to kick, cajole, or beat you into fulfilling His will. He will continue to woo and draw you but *it is your responsibility to respond.*

If you don't, then He will still love you. He will even take you to heaven. However, you won't ever birth His children in the earth. You won't be His voice to the lost, or be anointed to bind up the brokenhearted and bring deliverance to the captives.

CHAPTER 5 – THE WELL-BELOVED'S INSTRUCTIONS

SPEAKING TO OUR GOD-SHAPED VACUUM

The Beloved's response touches something deep in our souls. Blaise Pascal said, *"Inside every man there is a God-shaped vacuum and the whole life is empty until that vacuum is filled."*[1]

Augustine of Hippo said in his *Confessions*, "You have made us for yourself, O Lord, and our hearts are restless until they rest in You."

Allow God to fill that vacuum in your life. Then you can make sense of whatever life throws at you and put the pieces of life's puzzle in place.

He feeds His flock at noon.

The Beloved's response also sent the Shulamite woman back to her original questions:

> *"Tell me, O Thou whom My soul loveth, **where Thou feedest Thy flock**, where **Thou makest it to rest at noon**: for why should I be as one that [wandereth]?"*
> (Song of Solomon 1:7, bold emphasis mine)

We see three things that the Beloved does revealed in these questions posed by the Shulamite woman:

- **He causes the flock to lie down.** We know from Psalm 23, for instance, that the Good Shepherd causes us to lie down in green pastures, beside the still waters where His sheep may rest, eat, and drink their fill.

- **He does this at the noon hour.** Remember our insight from noted scholars Keil and Delitzsch concerning the Hebrew word translated as *noon*. It means "double light," referring to that time of day when the light of the sun directly overhead is so bright that there is ***no shadow*** visible. This is the ultimate metaphor or picture of transparency, vulnerability, and clarity.[2]

- **"I want to *know* You clearly."** The Shulamite's question, *"... why should I be as one that [wandereth]?"* expresses her desire to know Him clearly. The Beloved's answer reveals that He *may be so known* and draws her deeper!

*When doubts and distractions give way to intimacy, revelation is **inevitable**.* Our Shepherd promised in the Book of Hebrews:

> *"Now the God of peace, that brought again from the dead our Lord Jesus, that great shepherd of the sheep, through the blood of the everlasting covenant,*
>
> **"Make you perfect in every good work to do His will,** *working in you that which is well-pleasing in His sight, through Jesus Christ; to whom be glory for ever and ever. Amen."*
> (Hebrews 13:20–21. emphasis mine)

"Rest at noon"

The phrase "rest at noon" from Song of Solomon 1:7 describes that place of mature *trust* to which God wants us all to come.

This is a step beyond being fed and receiving gifts from the Beloved. *This is a movement into intimate rest for the soul.*

First, we must understand that the Soul is "accepted in the Beloved" from the very beginning.

Second, we are called into something *more* than acceptance. We are invited to "draw near with a true heart in full assurance of faith, having a heart *sprinkled* from an evil conscience" (to borrow the eloquence of Hebrews 10:22a). The Greek word translated as "sprinkled" is *hrantizo;* meaning "cleansed, purged, and purified."

CHAPTER 5 – THE WELL-BELOVED'S INSTRUCTIONS

He calls her "fairest among women" at this stage.

*"If Thou know not, **O thou fairest** among women…"*
(Song of Solomon 1:8a, italics mine)

The Beloved addresses her as "O thou *fairest.*" This passage used to bring up gender issues for me that really distracted me from the central message of God. Then I found the key I'm sharing in this book: *the Song of Solomon actually reveals the major steps of Christian maturity in God's Kingdom plan.*

DON'T BE DISTRACTED BY GENDER ISSUES.

Don't be distracted by gender issues—put a parenthesis around "women" to help get it out of your way if it helps. The principle is the same for women distracted by the extreme number of references to man, men, and mankind in the Scriptures where God is actually addressing *all* of His children, male *and* female.

This is the *first time* the Beloved speaks directly to the Shulamite. It is significant that in his first sentence he chooses to address her using a term that elevates her above all of the virgins around her!

Even though the Shulamite woman sees herself as "black," the Beloved calls her "thou *fairest.*"

Even as the Shulamite obsesses on her "blackness" the Beloved sees her heart and calls her "thou *fairest.*"

The Hebrew word used here means *to be bright, beautiful, handsome, and even "purged."*

First Samuel 16:7b says, "…the Lord seeth not as man seeth; for man looketh on the outward appearance, but the Lord looketh on the heart."

It is almost as if *the blacker the Shulamite is in her own eyes, the fairer she is in His!* Jessie Penn-Lewis imagined the Lord saying:

Oh soul, I will show thee the wonder,
The worth of My priceless blood;
Thou art whiter than snow on the mountains,
Thou art fair in the eyes of God.

The Lord Himself told a discouraged apostle, "My grace is sufficient for thee: for *My strength is made perfect in weakness*" (2 Corinthians 12:9a).

In answer to her desire for instruction, He directs her to go forth in the footsteps of the *flock* and continue her work among the shepherd's tents.

"If Thou know not, O thou fairest among women, *go thy way forth by the footsteps of the flock*, and *feed thy kids [the small sheep] beside the shepherd's tents*" (Song of Solomon 1:8, parenthetic insertion and italics mine).

The Beloved provided two key instructions that are vitally important to our transformation into the Bride of Christ today:

First, He did *not* ask her to *separate* from others.

The deepest walk with God is not monasticism. You can't become godly by yourself because God ordained for it to happen in community, in the body of Christ.

The Scriptures clearly say, "Not forsaking the assembling of ourselves together, as the manner of some is; but exhorting one another: and so much the more, as ye see the day approaching" (Hebrews 10:25).

CHAPTER 5 – THE WELL-BELOVED'S INSTRUCTIONS

You won't become any holier outside the body of Christ under a tree or in your living room. It's just not going to happen. In other words, you don't have to pull away and become a hermit to be holy!

The Beloved told the Shulamite, "Go thy way forth *by the footsteps of the flock.*" What does this mean for us today? He calls us to move forward as disciples while *"staying in the Family of God—the church."* Find the (Good) Shepherd's tent (household, family, church) where you belong and serve Him there in a god-like way.

Second, He did not call her to *cease* from her ministry or duties.

Holiness does not require all leisure. The Beloved told the Shulamite, "Feed thy kids beside the shepherd's tents."

He didn't say, "Stop all your ministry and work in the church." He was saying, "Balance it." You can be holy and drive a truck or work in an office eight hours a day. Paul did it while making tents!

He says to each of us on the journey, *"Do not withdraw from thy fellows and do not cease from thy service to others."*

THE KING'S VOICE: "OH, MY FRIEND."

*"I have compared thee, **O my [friend]**, to a company of horses in Pharaoh's chariots."*
    (Song of Solomon 1:9, insertion and bold emphasis mine)

The Beloved *continues* to speak to the Shulamite woman after He calls her "Fairest," and they are in *relationship*.

The King James Version and many other versions translate this passage as "O My love" because the Hebrew word used here is *"reyeh."*

Reyeh is often translated as "love," but it may also be translated as "friend" according to context. It is a feminine word so it would refer to a female friend.

Remember that we are dealing with a metaphor now, and everything about this passage is symbolic. We must work our way into the symbol to get the revelation, which is the goal of this book.

I believe He has just begun to speak because she has been talking too much.

Wilderness saints who love new experiences also talk a lot. They talk mostly about "What happened to *me*." They chiefly focus on how *they* feel and what *they* are doing.

By this point, however, the Shulamite is silent; and that is when *He* starts talking.

The Lord loves to hear us share with Him, talk about Him and worship Him. However, wonderful things happen when we finally get still in His presence: *"Be still,* and know that I am God" (Psalm 46:10b, italics mine).

The Beloved speaks cheerful words in response to the Shulamite woman's words.

When the Shulamite finally quiets down, He starts to speak cheerfully and even brags on her! He tells her things about herself that perhaps she didn't know (He does the same with us).

- *Young Mary* was a virtually unknown 13-year-old girl when an angel told her: "Hail, thou that art highly favoured, the Lord is with thee: blessed art thou among women" (Luke 1:28b). She gave birth to our Savior nine months later and the world has never been the same.

CHAPTER 5 – THE WELL-BELOVED'S INSTRUCTIONS

- *Gideon* was a frightened Israelite hiding from the Midianites in a winepress when the Angel of the Lord (probably the pre-incarnate Christ) said, "The Lord is with thee, thou mighty man of valor" (Judges 6:12). He delivered Israel from her enemies.

- *Moses* spent 40 years in Pharaoh's household as an adopted son, and another 40 years on the backside of the wilderness as a fugitive from Egypt, from God, and from his God-given responsibility. Yet God Himself spoke from a burning bush and said, "Moses, Moses, *Deliverer, deliverer*" (Moses' name in Hebrew is translated at times as "deliverer.") His stuttering response was essentially, "Who, me?" Yet he delivered Israel from Pharaoh's bondage, leader of one of the most powerful civilizations at the time.

Be quiet and still in His presence. Give Him time to talk when you pray, because He'll tell you things about yourself. (Then *you* can confess those things God confesses about you. Those two confessions spoken in agreement will "establish it forever" according to the precedent in 1 Chronicles 17:23.) Give God a chance to talk.

GIVE GOD TIME TO TALK WHEN YOU PRAY.

Notice that she recognizes His voice. It was Jesus who said, "My sheep hear My voice, and I know them, and they follow Me" (John 10:27).

She didn't have the benefit of this wisdom from Jesus in the New Testament. It seems from the context in the Song of Solomon, that she had never heard the Beloved speak directly to her before.

Yet, she recognized Him from the first word He said to her! She seemed to be saying, "Oh, that's my beloved. I can pick Him out in a crowd. I know when He's talking to me."

This is not a thing of the ears. It's a thing of the spirit. It is pictured in Psalm 42:7a, *"Deep calleth unto deep at the knowledge of thy waterspouts."* Remember that water represents the Holy Spirit throughout the Bible. This passage pictures the Holy Spirit billowing up from inside—*deep calling unto deep.*

At this stage of the union the Beloved seems to speak little and seldom. The "pouring forth" is all on the Shulamite woman's side as we noted earlier.

It is good that she is hungrier than all of the others present, so I don't want to criticize her (even though she does some dumb things while pursuing her relationship with the Beloved). However, the Shulamite's example teaches two things at this stage that may help you understand your own journey with the Lord:

1. *Her constant speaking is a sign that* **she is not in unbroken communion with Him**.

2. *She is "giddy but shallow" at this stage.* You know the deeper the water, the stiller it is on the surface. (Please don't consider this permission to be a "deadhead" in church! Remember God likes us hot or even cold, but He despises *lukewarm* attitudes according to Revelation 3:15-16).

"My soul followeth *hard* after Thee."
(Psalm 63:8a, emphasis mine)

David's statement perfectly describes the Shulamite's status at this stage: *in relationship with the Beloved,* and *getting close to the next stage.*

CHAPTER 5 – THE WELL-BELOVED'S INSTRUCTIONS

Jesus described the role of desire in Matthew 11:12, "And from the days of John the Baptist until now the kingdom of heaven suffereth violence, and the violent take it by force."

Jessie Penn-Lewis believed the original language suggested that the end of the verse read, "...*and those who have a* **vehement desire** *seize upon it.*"

THE SOUL REALLY WANTS A RELATIONSHIP WITH THE BELOVED.

This is an earnest pressing on – and pressing in – to ***know*** *the Lord, not merely* ***experience*** *Him.*

The Bible says, "[The Lord] made known His *ways* unto Moses, His *acts* unto the children of Israel" (Psalm 103:7, italic emphases mine). Intimacy affects revelation!

When my wife, Joanne, and I were first married, we went to a restaurant for dinner and observed an elderly couple dining together nearby. We were puzzled because throughout their meal they looked at each other but they didn't say much more than ten words the whole time.

I confidently told my new bride, "Darling, I will never be like that. I will always talk to you, Joanne. And if I don't, I want you to get on my case."

Today we know better. After spending many decades together, we now understand that those two married folks were communicating, but they didn't need chatter. She knew what he was thinking and he knew what she was thinking. They just weren't using words. As the saying goes, "Still waters run deep."

THE MAKING OF A BRIDE

God wants that kind of a relationship with us. If our faith in Him is shallow, we're noisy about it most of the time. When our faith is deeper, we don't have to be so noisy, so splashy.

William Law's writing influenced such 18th century leaders as Samuel Johnson, George Whitefield, and John and Charles Wesley. He wrote:

> "Thou canst go no faster than a full dependence on God can carry thee."

The Beloved encourages the Shulamite's hunger, but He also guides her progress for the greatest genuine growth.

> *"I have compared thee, O my [friend], to a company of horses in Pharaoh's chariots."*   (Song of Solomon 1:9, insertion mine)

The Beloved compares her to the beautiful, well-trained horses that pulled Pharaoh's chariots.

At this point in her journey, the Shulamite woman is just beginning Level 4 out of 12 levels. She is beginning to move into a *relationship* with the Beloved, and *the first thing He does is compare her to a horse!*

"Hello, Horsey." Do you know a woman who would respond well to that statement? The only way I can see it is if *the reference is actually a word picture or symbol of something much richer and more wonderful.*

The Song of Solomon is neither sexist nor erotic (unless your mind is in the gutter); it is symbolic. It is *agape* from start to finish, not *eros* love.

What could the Beloved possibly be referring to here?

CHAPTER 5 – THE WELL-BELOVED'S INSTRUCTIONS

He was alluding to *the famous Arabian horses that pulled Pharaoh's chariots in Egypt. They were the best-trained horses in the ancient world.* The Pharaohs of Egypt carefully developed the purest strains of the great Arabian horse, and this is where Solomon acquired his war horses against the command of God (see 2 Chronicles 1:16-17). He had "40,000 stalls of horses" for his chariots according to 1 Kings 4:26.

- *These Arabian horses were so eager to obey, that the slightest **touch** brought them to the task. They needed no whips or harsh jerks on their bridles.*

- The Beloved says of the Shulamite, *"You are as eager to please me as they [the Arabian mares] are to please Pharaoh."*

In other words, *her will is now surrendered. The slightest indication of direction is enough.* I sometimes joke that it takes us humans about 50 years to develop that kind of relationship. I'm thankful that my wife finally trained me well enough that she doesn't have to put a bridle on me and jerk me around anymore.

THE KING'S PROMISES

> *"Thy cheeks are comely with plaits of hair ... We will make thee plaits of gold with studs of silver."* (Song of Solomon 1:10-11)

The King makes His promise and any hint of "eroticism" goes out of the door! We've all heard of the "The Bearded Lady" circus acts common in smaller circuses, but I've never heard anyone describe hair growing out of a woman's cheeks as erotic—have you? Who wants a wife with a beard? I mean, not a huge beard, anyway.

The plaits of hair indicate attractive things about the purchased one from an *earthly* point of view.

THE MAKING OF A BRIDE

In the Bible, hair represents earthly beauty. Her *hunger* is "comely" or beautiful to Him. Even *the Shulamite's earthly and therefore imperfect efforts are satisfying to the Beloved at this stage.*

Elsewhere, we see that Absalom, David's son, was known for his long, flowing beautiful hair. Paul taught the early churches that a woman's long hair was her "glory" in First Corinthians 11:15.

The Beloved says, "We will take the earthly beauty embodied in your plaits of hair and we will make you plaits of gold." Gold represents divinity and Heaven rather than Earth. Secondly, He says in essence, "And I'm going to anchor them with studs of silver."

- *The Beloved promises that the earthly life will give place to the divine life implied by gold plaits.*
- *The beauty of braided earthly hair will give way to the beauty of plaited gold.* The earthly will give way to the heavenly.

This promise implies fire, because gold is most workable when it is subjected to heat. Gold hardly ever appears by itself in nature, it is usually bound up in rock or some other material. Raw gold ore, until the development of modern chemical techniques, was usually smelted or heated until the gold melted and separated from the rock, crystal, mineral, or metal ore holding it. It has been said that only when gold is purified by fire will it perfectly mirror what is closest to it.

God must melt us and separate us from what holds us before He can remake us; and so it was with the Shulamite woman. She moved out from among the other virgins and entered into a relationship with her Beloved. Now she must go through some fire to draw

CHAPTER 5 – THE WELL-BELOVED'S INSTRUCTIONS

even closer to Him. In the process of the fire He will transform her earthly beauty into heavenly beauty.

The symbolism of remaking or rebirth in the Song is incredible, isn't it?

This remaking of the earthly plaits of hair into plaits of gold must be anchored or secured by studs of silver.

When silver is mentioned in the Bible, it nearly always indicates redemption (as at Calvary).

God is going to transform the earthly things of her life into heavenly things *through her redemption*. Without exception, *the natural man must be redeemed before he can participate in the Divine Life.*

> *"**I am crucified with Christ: nevertheless I live; yet not I, but Christ liveth in me:** and the life which I now live in the flesh I live by the faith of the Son of God, who loved me, and gave himself for me."* (Galatians 2:20, italics mine)

The promise of the bridegroom also indicates a *crown* for the purchased one.

The crown is made of "borders of gold with studs of silver."

The "border" refers to the bottom of the crown.[3] The "studs of silver" are both decorative and practical. The upper arms or portions of the crown that come down the sides of the head are fastened and held together with studs of silver. Again, silver speaks of the *Redemption*. The complete picture is one of a gold crown anchored and adorned with the studs of silver.

When the heavenly bride reigns with Christ, this is the crown she will wear (Jesus promised crowns for overcoming churches comprising the Body and Bride of Christ in Revelation 2:10 and 3:11).

It rewards her deeds of redemption, accomplished *after being redeemed* by the Lamb.

Later on, you will discover that this is the same crown that is worn by the Bridegroom!

Jessie Penn Lewis quotes *Jamieson, Fausset, and Brown*, noting that "spouse" in Hebrew means a "crowned one."[4] The bride is the only one who can wear that crown. Virgins don't receive such a crown.

The surrendered Soul, "pressing toward the mark for the prize," is promised that the work will be accomplished.[5]

The Beloved gives the Shulamite two promises at this point:

1. She *shall* sit with Him in His throne of glory. We read in Revelation 3:21: *"To him that overcomes will I grant to sit with Me in My throne...."*

2. She *shall* know the divine life in union with Him. The Apostle Paul declared in Philippians 1:21, *"For me to live is Christ."*

The Shulamite woman is beginning to move into a legal relationship with Him that will ultimately make her His bride and earthly representative with full "power of attorney."

Again, Paul said it well: *"I live, yet not I, but Christ lives in me"* (Galatians 2:20).

Then we have the *third* promise expressed by the Beloved to the Shulamite:

3. *"We will make thee plaits of gold with studs of silver."*

Who is we? He is saying, "You and I will create this crown for you to wear as My bride. We will do that as you continue to

CHAPTER 5 – THE WELL-BELOVED'S INSTRUCTIONS

follow Me as I guide you in your growth." Now, that's what Christian life is all about.

God makes not two, but *three* promises, and He will perform them. Now, how will He do that?

Certain truths about God's character are timeless and transcend Old and New Covenant divisions. For instance, "If God says it, that settles it." We read in Numbers 23:19b: "Hath He said? And shall He not do it? Or hath He spoken, and shall He not make it good?" Psalm 138:2b declares, ". . . Thou hast magnified Thy Word above Thy Name."

He brings her now to the King's table at this Fourth Stage of development.

THE MAKING OF A BRIDE

End Notes – Fairest Among Women

1. Blaise Pascal, *Pensées VII* (425), in 1670 (published posthumously in 1672).

2. Keil and Delitzsch, "Proverbs, Ecclesiastes, Song of Solomon." *Commentary on the Old Testament*, Vol. VI.

3. *Gesenius' Hebrew-Chaldee Lexicon* notes that the Hebrew word, *tore*, translated as "border" in this passage, has two meanings. The first is *"order, row, turn, especially used of what goes round in a circle"* (Esther 2:12, 15). The second, from Song of Solomon 1:10, is *"a string of pearls,* or gold or silver beads (as an ornament for the head)".

4. Ibid, referring to the Hebrew root of bride, *kalal*, "to perfect," and its Arabic root, also notes the meaning "to put a crown upon, to crown."

5. See Philippians 3:14.

CHAPTER 6

STAIRSTEP 4 – CONTINUED
FAIREST AMONG WOMEN

THE KING'S TABLE

"'While the King sat at His table,' she says, 'my spikenard sent forth its fragrance. My Beloved is to me as a bundle of myrrh that lies betwixt my breasts.'"   (Song of Solomon 1:12–13)

The voice of the Lord restores calm and soothes the Shulamite woman with the knowledge that the King sits at His table in her heart.

Until this moment, **she had become occupied with self-revelation, spiritual self-accomplishment, and the misjudgment of her "mother's sons" (other Christians).** These were the things she worried about the most in the earlier stages.

When she turned to Him in her confusion and helplessness at Stage 4, it became her greatest step to that point. Sadly, many never go on from there.

Her helplessness is her **safety**, *because she truly can depend on Him.* If she had done like most and turned back to *her* ministry, *her* pursuit of blessings, and *her* holiness, then she would have substituted those for Him.

"And a highway shall there be, and a way, and it shall be called the way of holiness; the unclean shall not pass over it; but it shall be for those: the wayfaring men, though fools, shall err therein.

"No lion shall be there, nor any ravenous beast shall go up thereon, it shall not be found there; but the redeemed shall walk there.

"And the ransomed of the Lord shall return and come to Zion with Song and everlasting joy upon their heads: they shall obtain joy ..." (Isaiah 35:8-10a)

This is relationship, not just experiences in Him.

He is in charge of her life now. She can trust His *faithfulness*.

By coming into this vulnerable relationship with Beloved, her life becomes His responsibility as much or more than the Shulamite woman's. That is a good place to be. (It sure beats chasing "revival" all over town in search of a blessing.)

"When He giveth quietness, who then can make trouble?"
(Job 34:29a)

Her spikenard sends forth its fragrance.

Because the Beloved sits at the table in her heart, He also provides her heart everything that she needs. She doesn't need to chase blessings or drag her ministry around in circles so people will speak well of her (as Martha did in Luke 10:40).

Spikenard signifies *humility*, a grace only possible through His presence within. Now she is saying, "While He is ministering within my heart, my humility is growing."

Many people believe humility means, "I'm nothing to anybody," but that is the exact opposite of true humility.

Humility means that I can look at something and see it and accept it just as it is. The Shulamite is beginning to look beyond her blackness and *see Him* inside her, and with this new understanding she moves into a whole new dimension.

She is now becoming more focused on *them* and on *Him* than on herself. Soon she will be focused primarily upon Him. This is the path of growth for the soul in the Song of Solomon.

He sits at the table and she is filled with humility. This is a situation in which He *feeds* His beloved.

If you want to grow in Him, this is the way to get it done. He sits at table in your heart, and you humble yourself in His presence and allow Him to feed you. This is the "Mary Syndrome" in the Mary/Martha narrative of Luke 10:38-42.

Jesus pictures this perfectly when He says, "Behold, I stand at the door, and knock: if any man hear My voice, and open the door, *I will come in to him, and will sup* [eat dinner] *with him, and he with Me*" (Revelation 3:20, italic emphasis mine).

"My Beloved is to me as a bundle of myrrh that lieth betwixt my breasts." *(Song of Solomon 1:13)*

This fabulous statement has thrown more "curve balls" at Bible expositors than just about any other part of the Song of Solomon.

The problem with "breasts" in this passage disappears when Hebrew contextual idioms, metaphors, and allegories are recognized for what they are: they are *symbols* representing things far more important and far-reaching than a mere anatomical component.

God included this book in His Word because it addressed eternal Kingdom principles of redemption and relationship, not because we needed a sex manual.

THE MAKING OF A BRIDE

Remember that this scripture passage says through metaphor, "My Beloved is to me as a bundle of myrrh *that lies in my heart.*"

She declares that she is going to follow Him at all *costs*.

> "My Beloved is to me as a **bundle of myrrh** that lies betwixt my breasts." (Song of Solomon 1:13, emphasis mine)

A hidden treasure resides in the phrase, "a bundle of myrrh." One King James Version marginal note adds this phrase to increase our understanding: "a bundle of myrrh: yea, even as a *cluster of cypress.*"

It is ironic that the English word, **"campfire"** comes from an Old English root, *camphire*, referring to *cypress, a cypress tree or a fir tree.*

The next verse in Song of Solomon 1 reinforces this interpretation using a Hebrew term with incredible meaning and significance for us:

> "My beloved is unto me as a cluster of **camphire** in the vineyards of Engedi." (Song of Solomon 1:14, bold emphasis mine)

The Hebrew word translated "camphire" is *kopher,* referring to the Kopher tree. God commanded that the lid of the Ark of the Covenant be crafted of *kopher wood* and covered with a thin sheet of gold that had been melted and tamped down with no sound (see Exodus 40 and following).

The place on top of that gold-plated kopher lid between the golden seraphim was called "the mercy seat." It was known as the place of redemption.

It gets better.

Jesus our redeemer is called the *Kipporeth* in Hebrew. In other words, He is now our new Ark of the Covenant, our new place of redemption.

CHAPTER 6 – THE KING'S TABLE

This is my point: *all of this is about redemption*. The word, *Kopher*, is also the word *Kippur*. Does it sound familiar? *Yom Kippur* is the Hebrew name of the Day of Atonement. This day is celebrated on the Jewish calendar. All of this is symbolism pointing to redemption.

The Shulamite woman said, in effect, "He is a bundle of myrrh in my heart. I'm redeemed through His death and through His resurrection in my heart." The symbolism of this unusual book goes on and on.

Myrrh is both *expensive* and very, very *bitter*, and it is acquired by cutting through the bark of the *Commiphora Myrrha* tree.

Gum resin reservoirs under the bark of the Myrrh tree begin to seep from those cuts to form tear-shaped drops or beads that harden.

Verse 14 is talking about the cleft of the rock and *signifies death, bitterness and suffering*.

When the Shulamite woman says, "My Beloved, who sits at his table feeding me, is a bundle of myrrh in my heart that sends forth its fragrance," she is picturing our Beloved's sacrificial death on the Cross.

There is more!

Cypress is the funeral or cemetery tree of the east and it always signifies *death*.

In fact, Jesse Penn Lewis strongly implies that *both myrrh and cypress in the Scriptures signify death and are references to the Cross.*

As the Shulamite sits at the King's table, it begins to dawn on her through her Beloved's clues that she faces a higher cost in this union. Her response to Him reflects her stronger commitment.

THE MAKING OF A BRIDE

Perhaps it is no accident that most of the original scrolls of the Bible itself were written on *papyrus*.

Papyrus in Moses' era was a type of paper made from cypress wood or old cypress leaves that had been inundated by the Nile River. Cypress is naturally resistant to water, but eventually it begins to break down leaving behind only the hard bark.

Papyrus was gathered from those waters of death and spread out to dry in the sun. Then the material was beaten on one side until it was flattened enough to use as a writing surface. Scribes often used papyrus like this to record and preserve the Word of God.

It is all about **redemption**.

The question for you and me at this point in our own journey is this:

What will we say to the King Who sits at His table?

Jesse Penn Lewis provides two time-proven responses to the King from the Scriptures that will also anchor our own journey with the Lord:

"I will not leave Thee" (Elisha speaking to Elijah in 2 Kings 2:6b).

"My heart is fixed, O God ..." (David responding to God in Psalm 57:7a).

CHAPTER 7

STAIRSTEP 5
COMMUNION WITH HIM

DOVE
(DEVOTED IN THE BANQUETING HOUSE)

SONG OF SOLOMON 1:15-2:7

HUNGRY FOR MORE …

"Behold, **thou art fair, my** *[friend]; behold, thou art fair;* **thou hast doves' eyes."**
(Song of Solomon 1:15, italic emphasis mine)

When the Beloved tells the Shulamite, "*Behold, thou art fair; thou hast doves' eyes,*" He sees that her heart resembles the heart of David who said, "*My heart is fixed, Oh God*" (Psalm 57:7a).

The Hebrew word translated as "fixed" in this verse means "nailed," as in *"a nail driven into a tree."*

Once you drive a nail into a tree, you can kiss the nail goodbye because that tree will keep on growing until it encompasses and envelops the nail! The only way to separate the nail from the tree is to kill the tree.

THE MAKING OF A BRIDE

David said, "I have driven my love into you, God, as if I was driving a nail into a tree. I can never take it back again." (I hope that you respond to God in the same way!)

Chapter 7 brings us to the fifth of twelve steps of discipleship. This is the Beloved bringing the Shulamite into the banqueting house.

One New Testament passage in particular echoes the heart of the Lord revealed at this point in the Song:

> "The Master saith, where is My guest-chamber, where I shall eat ... with My disciples?"   (Mark 14:14)

It is here in the banqueting house that He says to her, "Behold thou art fair, My [love, my friend] ... *Thine eyes are as doves eyes.*"

He compares the Shulamite to a dove, and in this context dove means "devoted one." Now that is a step above mere relationship because it introduces *exclusivity* into the relationship.

When a relationship grows between two people in a human courtship, they begin to develop "doves' eyes" for each other. On a spiritual plane, that is a wonderful place to be with God.

THE WHISPER OF THE KING

The Beloved now sees the Holy Dove of the Spirit shining through the **eyes** *of the hungry, surrendered soul. "Dove's eyes" in a believer's life today reveal self-abandonment and* **trust** *in the Lord.*

The Shulamite's relationship with the Beloved is becoming intensified at this stage. *The Beloved looks at her and sees Himself reflected in her eyes.*

The Holy Spirit had brought her to this place of *yieldedness*.

CHAPTER 7 – DEVOTED

This is a place of vulnerability and yieldedness. Even in the natural or literal story of Solomon and the Shulamite Woman, there was no intercourse yet. That doesn't happen until she is a bride.

However, in this place of yieldedness, she is becoming totally His. She's not there yet, but she's getting there.

*Now, He moves on to enable her to be **single**-eyed in her devotion to Him.*

King David had this quality in his relationship with God. In fact, he revealed he was a "dove" in Psalm 27:4:

> *"One thing have I desired of the Lord, that will I seek after; that I may dwell in the house [face] of the Lord all the days of my life, to behold the beauty of the Lord, and to enquire in His temple."*
> *(Psalm 27:4, parenthetical insertion mine)*

A better translation from the original Hebrew context implies that David actually said: "…*that I may dwell in* **the face of my Lord**."

He was saying, "I want to be in God's face all of the days of my life. *I want Him to look into my eyes and I want to look into His eyes every day of my life.*"

Why did he do this? To "behold the beauty of the Lord, to inquire in His Temple" (*to seek out who He is*)!

Sadly, he didn't do it. He allowed distractions to pull his attention and affections elsewhere and it cost him big time.

Wade E. Taylor talks about dove's eyes in his book, *The Secret of the Stairs:*

> "A dove is similar to a pigeon, but a dove has one unique quality that no other bird has. It has a 'single eye.' That is, it has no side [or peripheral] vision. For this reason, doves

are often referred to as 'love birds.' This is because when one sets its gaze on another dove, its eye is 'single'—it sees nothing else, nor is it easily distracted."[1]

They will just gaze into one another's eyes over a dinner table or in a crowded room, totally transfixed with one another.

When I share this in public or classroom settings, I don't look to younger listeners for confirmation and echoed experiences. I look for people who have lived long enough to experience this deeper form of love.

The Shulamite is approaching this place of intimacy at this stage. The Beloved is drawing her closer with words of enduring affection. What is her response?

THE RESPONSE OF THE SOUL

> "Behold, thou art fair, my love; behold, thou art fair; thou hast doves' eyes." (Song of Solomon 1:15)

Remember that whenever you see a statement like this addressed to "my love," "my friend," or "my dove"; it is addressed to the Shulamite woman or metaphorically to the Bride of Christ.

On the other hand, when you see a statement addressed to "my Beloved," then it is addressed to Solomon in the narrative or metaphorically to the Bridegroom of the Church, Jesus Christ.

The Shulamite speaks in response now:

TRUE WORSHIP MAKES LIFE RICHER AND FULLER.

> "Behold, thou art fair, my beloved, yea, pleasant (nayim): also **our** bed (couch) is green.
>
> "The beams of **our** house are cedar, and **our** rafters of fir (cypress).

CHAPTER 7 – DEVOTED

"I am the rose of Sharon, and the lily of the valleys"
(Song of Solomon 1:16—2:1, insertions and bold emphasis mine).

Notice that she *returns* all of the praise that He has just heaped on her.

She knows that her only beauty is His Presence within her—she has none apart from *Him*.

Isn't this a wonderful place to come? Doesn't this beat traipsing around all over the county "looking for the fire"? Doesn't this beat "hunting manna" from church to church and community to community?

It is all of grace.

It is all of *Him*.

She doesn't isolate herself in a cave by herself or ignore the shepherd's instruction. She stays with the flock and she raises the young lambs by the shepherd's tent under His authority. She's in the church and in the body, but she's growing in Him.

She is growing in her understanding of her Beloved.

Before this stage, she was focused on what she received from Him, whether it took the form of a blessing, a ministry, or even a greater level of holiness.

Then, "I" was dominant in her thought, not "Him."

Now, she ventures to say *our* couch, *our* house, and *our* rafters.

What magnificent symbolism: the Shulamite speaks of "our bed" or our couch, which is to say, "our place of embrace." Let me put it into a modern spiritual context:

"Also, our worship is productive. It is alive, verdant, and fruit bearing. I can tell the difference in my life since I started worship-

ing and loving You. My life is richer and fuller. It's not empty and dry and lifeless anymore."

Now she is beginning to realize it is not about "her." She moves her focus from "me" to "us" (but not yet solely to "Him.") She's not yet to "You" (the Beloved), which is where she's headed and where we must go. At the very least, she is no longer focused on herself.

She is growing in her Beloved.

More than 900 years later, *the Apostle Paul described this principle in his letter to early believers in the city of Corinth*:

> "All things are yours ... and ye are Christ's and Christ is God's." (1 Corinthians 3:21-23)

At this point the Shulamite woman begins to reply to Him, returning the praise of her Beloved. She knows that her only beauty comes from His presence within her. It's all of grace, and it's all of Him.

She has graduated from "me, my and I" to "our." She speaks of *our* couch, *our* house, and *our* rafters.

Her reference to fir or cypress shows that she is beginning to understand that union with the Beloved – the risen, glorified Christ – is based on fellowship with Him in His *death*.

We can't live His life until we die His death. You can't get to Easter except through Good Friday. You must go through the crucifixion to reach the resurrection.

We all want the resurrection. At least, we think we do. And we can get real noisy about it, but we're not too noisy about that crucifixion part. Paul told the believers in Rome:

CHAPTER 7 – DEVOTED

*"For if we have been planted together in the likeness of His death, we shall be also in the likeness of His **resurrection**."*
(Romans 6:5, emphasis mine)

Only one door leads to the new life in Christ described in Romans 6, and that is the door of death in Him. Why does the Shulamite's mention of fir trees matter today?

The cypress tree grows in the necropolis, a word meaning "the city of the dead."

Necropolis is a compound word based on the Greek terms *nekros* (the Greek word for "dead"), and *polis* (the Greek word for "city"). The cypress flourishes in the cemetery.

This reflects an underlying theme of Scripture and of spiritual life: *death to the old life* **and** *resurrection into the new.* We see it again and again from Genesis to Revelation in the Bible.

"Thou art fair, My Beloved.... I am (but a rose of Sharon –KJV) ... a lily of the valleys."   (Song of Solomon 2:1)

The Shulamite woman says, *"Thou art fair, my Beloved."* Remember that the Beloved has just said to her, *"Thou art fair, my love."*

Also remember that "fair" in this passage means, "You are translucent, you are open and apparent." She is saying, "I'm beginning to understand you. You're not a mystery to me anymore."

In fact, God is always a mystery to us because He is always more than we can understand. Yet, the Shulamite woman *is* beginning to learn how to relate correctly to Him (and so can we).

What a discovery!

It takes you from feeling as if your life is a confused mess to filling that "God-shaped vacuum" of the heart and seeing the puzzle pieces of life begin to fall into place one by one.

THE MAKING OF A BRIDE

The Soul is speaking of *herself*.

Some commentators say this expression is used of the Bridegroom (half agree with this and half do not). *I don't agree.*

I am convinced *the Shulamite woman is calling herself a Rose of Sharon and a lily of the valley* for several reasons.

A Rose of Sharon is a flesh-colored wild flower with a leafless stem. These wild plants fill the valleys of Galilee in one of the most verdant and green parts of Israel.

I've been in those valleys in the spring when the Roses of Sharon cover their slopes in waving, multicolored vistas blowing in the wind. It was as if they were literally praising God. It was incredible.

We are not talking about *the lush red, yellow and white roses that you and I know as roses that we send to people we love. They didn't come until much, much later and they are of Persian origin.*

Keil and Delitzsch say the term Sharon describes two things: "a meadow [*and a*] flower of Sharon."

These are wild flowers that don't cost anything. Some people might even consider them so common that they are worthless. These lilies of the valley, the Roses of Sharon, just grow up wild.

For these reasons, **this mention of the Rose of Sharon** *fits more accurately if the Soul uses it of* **herself.**

Consider the words of Jesus in Matthew 6:

> "And why take ye thought for raiment? **Consider the lilies of the field**, how they grow; they toil not, neither do they spin:
>
> "And yet I say unto you, That even Solomon in all his glory was not arrayed like one of these.

CHAPTER 7 – DEVOTED

> "Wherefore, if God so clothe the grass of the field, which to day is, and to morrow is cast into the oven, shall He not much more clothe you, O ye of little faith?
>
> "Therefore take no thought, saying, What shall we eat? or, What shall we drink? or, Wherewithal shall we be clothed?
>
> "(For after all these things do the Gentiles seek:) for your heavenly Father knoweth that ye have need of all these things.
>
> "But seek ye first the kingdom of God, and His righteousness; and all these things shall be added unto you.
>
> "Take therefore no thought for the morrow: for the morrow shall take thought for the things of itself. Sufficient unto the day is the evil thereof." (Matthew 6:28-34, emphasis mine)

Jesus is quoting the Song of Solomon in this passage, referring directly to Solomon in comparison to the "lily of the valley." The Bible says, "Out of the abundance of the heart the mouth speaketh" (Matthew 12:34b). Jesus was filled with the truths that saturate the Song of Solomon.

The Shulamite's reply to the Beloved was saying, "In and of myself, I'm just a worthless weed. But you have made me a lily of the valley and a Rose of Sharon."

This is the key. She is learning this.

THE KING'S ESTIMATE OF HIS FRIEND

> "As a lily among **thorns**, so is My love [friend] among the daughters." (Song of Solomon 2:2, insertion and italic emphasis mine)

The Beloved speaks in verse 2, and we once again see the Hebrew word, *reyeh*, translated in the King James Version as "*love*." Again, we will adopt the more contextually correct translation of "**friend**."

THE MAKING OF A BRIDE

He picks up the Shulamite's modest description of herself and affirms it:

"Thou art to My eyes a lily among *thorns*."

In other words, *she is a fragile and beautiful thing growing among thorn bushes.* Even at this stage she battles feelings of worthlessness, but He sees her as a beautiful lily among thorns.

While this is a compliment to the bride, notice that it is *not* directed toward the virgins.

What happens when you are right there with Him where He is present and available to you—but you just won't go there, you won't draw closer?

The answer is that you become prickly, thorny, and hard to get along with. Things don't work right and you feel out of sorts because even though the supposed object of your love is right there with you, and even though he offers everything that you could ever desire, *you just can't develop the hunger.*

Think of a child who fills up on chips and cheap candy just before a fabulous 4-course meal is served. There is no hunger for what his body truly needs.

He sees His own life and spirit growing in *her*.

Keil and Delitzsch say that *"…He sees her quiet life and finds her beautiful."*

This is happening even in the middle of the hardening, embittering and withering of the *others* around her.

Sadly, most churches are comprised of 90% virgins and only 10% brides. We shouldn't be surprised that sometimes the very same thing that melts the bride will anger the virgins!

CHAPTER 7 – DEVOTED

"We don't need that kind of people in our church. They're not like us. They need to go down to the other church down there, on the other side of the tracks."

When you hear this kind of chatter, you know that is a spiritual virgin talking, not a bride.

The *earth*-life can produce only thorns.

Paul describes these thorns in First Corinthians 3:12 as *"wood, hay and stubble."*

When the abundance of the deeper life in Christ is available to you but you don't choose it, you get "thorny."

> *"But that which beareth thorns and briers is rejected, and is nigh unto cursing; whose end is to be burned."*
> (Hebrews 6:8)

Notice the Bible doesn't say it was cursed, the passage says it is "nigh unto cursing." It's sad to admit that you can't pick out some virgins from worldlings, and you can't differentiate some Christians from non-Christians. They are olive trees that look so much like thorn bushes that you can't tell them apart.

In Song of Solomon 2:2, the Shulamite woman was flourishing even in the middle of a thorny atmosphere. *You don't need a hot church in order to be a hot Christian, and you don't need a happening church to be a happening saint!* The Shulamite flourished and became a lily of the valleys, a Rose of Sharon, while surrounded by thorn bushes.

> YOU DON'T NEED A HOT CHURCH TO BE A HOT CHRISTIAN.

After the Beloved shares His estimate of her, she learns to repeat what He says about her. In other words, she's learning the power of *confession*.

The Greek word that describes this action of "speaking the same words" is *homologia*." It is pronounced **ha**-ma-la-**gee**-ah, not "homo-logia."

Homo (pronounced *ha-ma*) means "the same as," *not* "similar." *Logia* means "sayings." Special things happen when you start saying about yourself the same things He is saying.

Yet, how can you do that unless you shut up and let Him talk?

Let Him talk to you.

Then you say back to Him what He is saying to you.

Confess the covenant. Pray the covenant. Believe what He says.

Remember that the greatest miracle of all time occurred when a 13-year-old virgin repeated the words of God, saying: "Be it unto me according to Thy word."

If you let Him talk, then you, too, can birth what He says.

God created everything by the word of His power. *And God said, and it was so.*

On the other hand, if you never let Him speak then it is probable that you will never amount to anything.

THE SOUL'S ESTIMATE OF HER BELOVED

"As the apple tree among the trees of the wood, so is my beloved among the sons. I sat down under His shadow ... His fruit was sweet to my taste." (Song of Solomon 2:3)

She compares her Beloved to a fruitful tree—an *apple tree*.

As her focus sharpens and becomes more fixed upon the Beloved, her responses and descriptions of Him become richer, deeper, and more detailed.

CHAPTER 7 – DEVOTED

Then she finds two things in Him: *sweetness* and *sustenance*.

An apple is *sweet* and *pleasant* (she said, "*His fruit is sweet to my taste*"). It is also *sustaining* and it provides *strength*.

English-speaking mothers and grandmothers have quoted this proverb to children for more than a century: "An apple a day keeps the doctor away." Science seems to agree that apples have a number of medicinal and nutritional properties. So does the Lord's presence.

The Beloved's presence provided the Shulamite with *shade*, *comfort* and *protection*. She said, "Under His shade I sat down." You could also say, "I sat down under His canopy or cover of *comfort*." It is a shade of *protection*.

He is now becoming all she needs:

- *Protection* (He is her shade and cover)
- *Pleasantness* (He is sweet to her taste)
- *Provision* (He is her sustenance and strength).

Once she was divided, looking to others or personal holiness for her consolation.

The carnal believers in the first century church at Corinth did the same thing when they claimed allegiance to personalities in leadership:

> "*Now this I say, that every one of you saith,* **I am of Paul;** *and* **I of Apollos;** *and* **I of Cephas;** *and* **I of Christ.** *Is Christ divided?*"   (1 Corinthians 1:12-13a, emphasis mine)

The Corinthians were immature and carnal or fleshly, and they demonstrated it when *they divided into "camps" and elevated their favorite "heroes"* among church leadership.

THE MAKING OF A BRIDE

*Now she begins to find **Him** her all in all,* the source of everything she needs.

INSIDE THE "BANQUETING HOUSE"

> *"As the apple tree among the trees of the wood, so is my beloved among the sons. I sat down under His shadow with great delight, and His fruit was sweet to my taste.*
>
> *"He brought me to the banqueting house, and His banner over me was love."* (Song of Solomon 2:3-4)

Notice that immediately after the Shulamite expanded her praise and vision of the Beloved ... Boom! He transports her to a new place and a transformed relationship.

> *"He brought me to the banqueting house, and His banner over me was love."*

The Soul is now entering into rest and *intimacy* with her Beloved.

Understand that when you talk about the banqueting house, it's one word in Hebrew: *yayin*. It means *wine, the house of wine*, not "banquet."

What does this mean? It obviously refers to the *rest, security, trust, joy,* and *vulnerability* afforded by **intimacy**.

INTIMACY
—
IN-TO-ME-SEE

I love the word, *intimacy*. Here's the way I spell it to help me remember its most important meaning: *IN-TO-ME-SEE*.

This is what we mean: "Come into me and see what I will do."

*Here she receives a foretaste of the **union** that she seeks with Him as He fills up her vision. It happens in the house of wine, the yayin.*

CHAPTER 7 – DEVOTED

This is where she receives *"joy unspeakable and full of glory"* (see 1 Peter 1:8).

The spiritual manifestation of the Beloved (the Risen Christ) in the heart is love. You can also declare that in Christ, "His banner over me is love."

> "But when it pleased God, who separated me from my mother's womb, and called me by His grace,
>
> "To reveal his Son in me, that I might preach Him among the heathen; immediately I conferred not with flesh and blood."
> (Galatians 1:15-16)

It has now "pleased God to reveal His Son in her." Incredible.

*This revelation is even **greater** than the "table revelation" of the Beloved as "gift-giver and provider" earlier in the Song.*

When Song of Solomon 2:4 says "the banqueting house" it is actually referring to the bedchamber or bedroom. What she eats there is not His food, it is Him in a sense.

The King James Version misses it here because the English language misses it. We hear or read "banqueting house" and immediately see Ezell's Fish House or Jeremy's All-You Can Eat Chinese Buffet.

No, this is the *yayin* house, the house of intimacy with Him.

Earlier in the Song, the Beloved *sat at His table* in her life, providing her with everything that she needed. "It is great to be redeemed. Look at all He gives me. It is wonderful."

This is much better; it is a whole stage beyond.

In the *yayin* house of intimacy, the Beloved doesn't give her *His gifts*. He enfolds her beneath His love into union with *Himself*.

THE MAKING OF A BRIDE

- Earlier, when He sat at table in her heart, He gave her what was *His*.
- Now, He gives her *Him*.

Do you see the difference? Not *His* ... but *Him*!

In the very next verse, we see the Shulamite woman completely miss the mark! Honestly, she very much reminds me of myself when she says:

> "Stay me with flagons, comfort me with apples: for I am sick [for] love." (Song of Solomon 2:5)

The King James Version translates this phrase as, "I'm sick *of* love." This older translation is accurate most of the time, but in this instance the translators missed it somehow.

According to the KJV reading, the Shulamite was telling the Bridegroom or Beloved at this point, "I don't need you. I have everything I need. I have all of your gifts, the flagons, and the wines. You can go and do whatever you want to until I get hungry."

No, this translation missed it by 180 degrees. All you have to do is change the preposition to get the correct reading. *According to Keil and Delitzsch, the Shulamite woman was "sick **for** love."*

The Shulamite wasn't sick *of* love, she was sick *for* love. She wanted more! However, she *still missed it*.

She told her Beloved, "*Stay* me with *flagons*." The Hebrew word translated as "stay" is *samak*. It means "to sustain, establish, or hold."

The Hebrew word translated in the King James Version as "flagons" is *ashiyshah*. *It refers to raisin cakes that were usually used*

CHAPTER 7 – DEVOTED

in sacrificial feasts. They were made from grapes that were dried and pressed into form.

According to 2 Samuel 6:19, "David fed the people flagons when he brought the ark into Jerusalem."

After the momentous return of the Ark of the Covenant to Jerusalem, King David helped the people celebrate with flagons or raisin cakes. You and I might call it "date-nut bread."

The Shulamite was saying, "Bring me some more raisin cakes. Let's eat and drink some wine." She wanted to stay there in the *yayin*, lingering in His embrace so the pleasure of intimacy would never end.

That's wonderful, but there is a place in God that is greater than our worship.

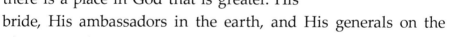

THERE IS A PLACE IN GOD THAT IS GREATER THAN OUR WORSHIP.

That is a shocking statement, but it is true!

I am a worshiper. I love to worship. Yet, there is a place in God that is greater. His bride, His ambassadors in the earth, and His generals on the planet must learn to go there.

*The Shulamite soaks up His intimacy and forgets everything else except **worship**.* She was saying, "Give me some more date-nut bread and wine and let's worship."

"His left hand is under my head, and with His right hand doth He embrace me" (Song of Solomon 2:6).

This word picture confounds more people than anything else because *this is a picture of intimacy between a husband and wife.* They are in an intimate embrace making love, if you will.

He pours His love into her.

THE MAKING OF A BRIDE

This is a picture of intimate worship.

She says in essence, "I want to stay here." What does the Beloved say?

THE WORD OF THE BELOVED

> "I adjure [charge – KJV] you, daughters of Jerusalem by the roes, and the hinds in the field that ye stir not up, nor awake my love, until it please." (Song of Solomon 2:7)

The King James Version says, "...nor awake my love until *it* please." This implies that it means "until *He* please."

Keil and Delitzsch provide what I feel is the proper contextual translation of this passage: "...arouse not and disturb not love 'til *she* pleases (is ready for the next level)."

He is saying, "Leave her alone until *she* gets her fill of worship and is ready to go forward."

God is growing her root system so that He can build a great edifice or significant structure of ministry, life, and influence on top of it.

This is the first of four statements in the Song that are mistranslated in ways that confuse their context and meaning. The remaining three passages are:

- *Song of Solomon 3:5*

  "I charge you, O ye daughters of Jerusalem, by the roes, and by the hinds of the field, that ye stir not up, nor awake my love, till he [she] please."

- *Song of Solomon 5:8*

  "I charge you, O daughters of Jerusalem, if ye find my beloved, that ye tell Him, that I am sick of [for] love."

CHAPTER 7 – DEVOTED

- *Song of Solomon 8:4*

  "I charge you, O daughters of Jerusalem, that ye stir not up, nor awake my love, until he [she] please."

These daughters typify the virgins, the other believers and workers who know *nothing* of this spiritual fellowship and union with the Beloved.

The "daughters" in these passages represent metaphorically "believers who minister to, get blessed by, and love the Bridegroom but are *not* the Bride."

I believe that 90 percent of preachers are virgins, and 90-to-95 percent of the church is composed of virgins. They are there because they are doing something, they are learning something, or they are feeling something that is His.

It is wonderful, and better than anything anywhere else. However, unless it is *Himself* and not merely *His*, then it can become an impediment to growth and an obstacle to progress rather than the cause of them.

The Beloved sees the "daughters" (of duty, work and ministry) ready to intrude and "stir up" this Soul and prevent God's time of *rest* (intimacy).

Judas was a virgin but not a bride at the last supper, even though he was one of the Twelve disciples of the Lamb![2] When Mary broke the alabaster box of precious perfume and poured all of her life savings on the feet of Jesus in selfless worship, Judas came in and said, *"What means this waste?"*

Such worship is waste to a virgin, but never to a bride.

THE MAKING OF A BRIDE

Judas did his best to prevent Mary's intimate worship and memorial with Jesus. It seems some of the other disciples also slipped into virgin mode that day as well.[3]

Modern-day virgins in the Church might say, *"We must stay busy...we don't have time for worship!"*

For such Christians, "Duty trumps devotion!"

Remember the words of Jesus in Matthew 11:28:

"Come unto Me, all you who labor and are heavy laden, and I will give you rest."

*Please, do not feel **guilty** for these wonderful times of intimate rest with the Lord.* Don't let anybody make you feel guilty about that.

However, there will come a time when He Himself will stir your nest to take you beyond just your worship.

During these special times, He Himself becomes the jealous keeper of His purchased one.

It is the *Beloved* who speaks so sternly to the virgins on behalf of the Shulamite woman:

"I charge you, O ye daughters of Jerusalem, by the roes, and by the hinds of the field, that ye stir not up, nor awake my love, till [she] please." (Song of Solomon 2:7, insertion mine)

He says to all of them, "Don't you dare intrude." I read one commentator discussing the phrase, *"His banner over me is love,"* who said that when the Beloved took the Shulamite into the chamber, He put this banner across the door to say, in essence, "No entrance. Occupied."

CHAPTER 7 – DEVOTED

Since she said, "Draw me; we will run after Thee" (Song of Solomon 1:4), He has tested her surrender and shown her more and more what it means to truly know the Lord."

The Shulamite has a strength of will and a stability of purpose now that she didn't have earlier.

Now He must lead her on to deeper tests and greater union, but He is going to lead her **gently***, for God is the master teacher.*

A master teacher operates differently from teachers with less vision, wisdom, and experience.

Dr. Earl Pullias was my mentor at the University of Southern California, School of Education. He was a founding faculty of the Department of Higher Education there, and was a friend to my family.

Although my father died before I met Dr. Pullias, they were two expressions of the same kind of soul and I loved them both dearly. Dr. Pullias was a great man and he became a father to me.

I'd finished my PhD in New Testament studies at USC and was teaching New Testament Exegesis in another college. During a transitional period in my life Dr. Pullias sucked me back to USC.

He talked me into getting into an MA program and then an EDD program, but the only reason I did it is because I wanted and needed to be with him because he had become a father to me.

He was one of the greatest men I've ever known. U.S. Vice presidents, Albert Einstein, and many other great people used to come to USC to speak for Dr. Pullias' "Town and Gown" meetings.

He wrote a landmark book entitled, *A Teacher Is Many Things*, featuring 26 vignettes or pictures of what a real teacher is. In Chapter 2, he described a great teacher as a guide who will take his students on a journey as far as they can go. He builds them a fire where they finally stop and warms them with the truth that they know.

While they are enjoying the fire, perhaps with marshmallows, cookies and Cokes, he will strike out alone in the middle of the night to stake out the path for the next day's journey.

He finds the place where he wants them to be, knowing they are capable of reaching that point. There he will build a bigger and better fire. After marking the path, he returns to his students clustered around the old campsite and begins to talk to them about the new place. His goal is to convince them to put out their existing fire.

He doesn't just kick out the fire and say, "Come on with me." That is the way of a dictator, not a teacher.

Instead, he tells them so much about the new place that they say by their own choice, "Let's go there!" Then *they* douse the fire and willingly follow his trail to the next place.

This is the way a true shepherd and great teacher works, and this is what the Song of Solomon is all about. This is the way the Bridegroom gently leads His Bride in the path He wants her to go.

He provides her this precious time of rest before He calls her to go deeper.

This is the reason He says, "I charge you, O daughters, don't stir up, don't awaken love until [she] pleases."

David describes God's intimate knowledge of our limitations and weaknesses in Psalm 103:14, "*He knoweth our frame; He remembereth that we are dust.*"

CHAPTER 7 – DEVOTED

The prophet Habakkuk, sounded a warning about worship when he declared, *"The LORD is in His holy temple: be silent before Him"* (Habakkuk 2:20). In other words: *When it presents itself, do not ignore or despise "worship time."*

King David weighed in again with a powerful psalm describing the comfort and security God's people find in Him when they stay close to Him:

> *"There is a river, the streams whereof shall make glad the city of God, the holy place of the tabernacles of the most High.*
>
> *"God is in the midst of her; she shall not be moved ..."*
> (Psalm 46:4-5a)

The Beloved wants us to let our roots grow deep in Him, and He wants us to enjoy the revelation that we have. Neither one of those things happens in a hurry.

So He says, in the Jessie Penn-Lewis version:

"I charge you, O daughters…that ye stir not up, nor awaken love until *she* please."

The Hebrew word translated as "please" is **chaphets** *(pronounced kah-fates'). It means "desirable, feasible or appropriate."*

He is saying is, *"When she is ready, he will move forward and deeper."*

Do you remember *William Law's* quote we mentioned earlier? *"Thou canst go no faster than a full dependence on God can carry thee."*

If you are a teacher or a leader in the church seeking to draw people closer to God and deeper into His presence, "Don't kick out the fire until they are ready to go forward." Follow the example of our Master Teacher.

THE MAKING OF A BRIDE

As you follow in the footsteps of Christ, you can be sure that God will not "jerk you out of joint" to get you to grow up in Him. He loves you as you are, "warts and all."

Yes, He'll keep you like you are, warts and all.

He will even take you to heaven just as you are, warts and all.

But, oh, how much better for you and for your children to be ready for His coming with the right everlasting fuel (like the wise virgins) at the place where He knows you need to be.

The Good Shepherd *leads* us, He does not *drive us*.[4]

As for the Shulamite woman, God is the Master Teacher. He knows *there is more that she must learn before she knows Him fully.*

CHAPTER 7 – DEVOTED

End Notes

1. Wade E. Taylor, *The Secret of the Stairs* (Salisbury Center NY: Pinecrest Publications, 1988). Parenthetical insertion mine.
2. See John 12:4-8.
3. See Matthew 26:6-9 and Mark 14:1-5.
4. See Ephesians 2:14 and John 17:23.

THE MAKING OF A BRIDE

CHAPTER 8

STAIRSTEP 6
SURRENDER TO HIM

SEPARATED (VULNERABLE)

SONG OF SOLOMON 2:8-13

"The voice of my beloved! Behold, He cometh leaping upon the mountains, skipping upon the hills.

"My beloved is like a roe or a young hart [deer]: behold, He standeth behind our wall, He looketh forth at the windows, shewing Himself through the lattice"
    (Song of Solomon 2:8-9, KJV, emphasis and insertion mine)

THE SOUL RESTING IN HER BELOVED SUDDENLY HEARS HIS VOICE AND RECOGNIZES IT AT ONCE.

The time has come when He senses she is able to move *forward*. Things dramatically shift and the Shulamite suddenly realizes it when she hears her Beloved's voice in a new way.

Her description of him no longer includes references to him as "a *gazelle* at rest" or lying in a prone position. She sees him "leaping upon the mountains, skipping upon the hills" – *outside* of her intimate chamber.

THE MAKING OF A BRIDE

"The Beloved now manifests Himself to her as the *risen* Lord." (Jessie Penn-Lewis)

It is as if He were calling from some distance away from her and not right there within her heart. He is a fast-moving gazelle awaiting her response to come away with Him for something more!

Now He is gently "stirring her up" to move *beyond the chamber* and into the *wilderness*.

Wait a minute! Aren't we supposed to be leaving the wilderness to enter the Promised Land? Don't we want to move from the outside to the inside? *How could this be progress?*

He has revealed Himself to her as the *indwelling One*. In the process, He also helped her learn the lessons of vulnerability:

- It is better to be *clear* or transparent with Him than to be outwardly *clean*.

- *Integrity* or honesty is better than preserving a false *innocence*.

- It is better to be *pliable* in His hands than pretend to be *perfect* in ourselves. We must quickly learn that perfection is something we can never achieve.

> BETTER TO BE PLIABLE THAN PRETEND TO BE PERFECT.

Best of all, she also learned how to worship.

For a season, the Beloved kept the Shulamite to Himself for a time of joyous rest and *intimacy*, building her up and giving her strength.

However, she is about to discover what all of us must learn; that *God knows when "our engine needs a tune-up."*

CHAPTER 8 – VULNERABLE

Now she must be brought to a deeper place of trust in Him alone, apart from His conscious revelations to her heart.

What is meant by His "conscious revelations" to her heart?

Her faith must rest upon Him alone, His *character* and His *word*, not His *manifestations*.

He "manifests" or reveals Himself to us in many ways, and some of them are so exciting that we may be tempted to focus more on His gifts and "manifestations" than upon Him.

Maturity resists that temptation. A mature faith rests on Him alone, and not merely upon His *blessings, His miracles, or even His "manifest presence."*

Basically, He exists and is worthy of our faith *whether or not we can feel or sense His presence.* I can relate to this as a husband who made a solemn marriage covenant with my wife. I understand that I should love my wife all the time—even when I don't feel like it or when I am far from her "felt" presence.

She must care more for *Him* than His *vineyards* and *works*, or His *chambers* and *blessings*.

Examine the life of Job and you will understand this statement! One verse especially seems to illustrate this level of caring for the Beloved more than all of His gifts, blessings, and benefits.

Job made this declaration *after* experiencing the removal of virtually all of his earthly blessings and benefits for reasons he did not understand: "Though He slay me, yet will I trust in Him" (Job 13:15a).

She must know that conformity to His *likeness* is more than ministry and rejoicing.

It is deeper than fleeting *feelings* and emotions.

It is even deeper than *knowing* Him or having deep revelation about Him.

It is more than *doing* things for Him such as ministry.

It is deeper than *having* or possessing things such as holiness or salvation.

It is *being one with Him*.

THE ATTITUDE OF THE RISEN LORD

"My beloved is like a roe or young hart [deer or gazelle]: behold, He standeth behind our wall, He looketh forth at the windows, He sheweth Himself through the lattice." (Song of Solomon 2:9)

The Risen Lord comes from *without* to draw her attention beyond her blessed experience *within*.

Don't be surprised to discover that *God puts Himself* and all that He is to us at any given time—His Presence, His provision, His comfort, His gifts—not where we *are*, but where He *wants us to be*!

The Psalmist ended his powerful psalm on unity with a promise to those who obey the instruction of the Lord: "For ***there*** the Lord commandeth the blessing!" (Psalm 133:3, emphasis mine).

We often use the phrase, "The place called *there*," to describe any place, position, or situation where we obey God's commands, follow His leading, or dare to step out in trust and faith. The Shulamite is about to discover her "place called there."

She is still lost in wonder over her time of intimacy with Him when she suddenly sees Him *outside* of the chamber! *She sees Him looking in, not out.*

She sees Him as a gazelle who is *standing*.

CHAPTER 8 – VULNERABLE

Her *new vision* of Him prepares her for *transition*. He is no longer *sitting* at a table bringing her gifts or meeting her needs through His blessings. Nor is He *lying* in a bedchamber providing intimacy and delight in worship.

In other words, there is something *even better* beyond the wall of worship, intimacy and surrender.

Her Beloved is no longer in the bedchambers, He is a fast-moving gazelle standing and awaiting her response to "come away with Him" for something *more*.

He stands and waits. Will she rise to the challenge to "come away" to the unknown? He beckons her to move to the next level of communion with Him!

She sees Him standing "behind our *wall*"

Most of us automatically assume the wall of the bedchamber was there to keep them in and everybody else out, yet the Beloved suddenly shows up calling from outside of the wall.

Do you remember my mentor's description of a great teacher preparing his students for the next level? This passage in the Song reveals the Beloved leading the Shulamite woman to a new level.

He is *outside* — on the other side of intimacy, beyond the wall of worship and holiness. For the first time, *she sees Him in times of intimacy speak to her of sacrificial service.*

> "Will you sacrifice some of your precious times
> of intimacy with Me in service to others?"

What is going on? She sees Him looking in (not "out"), and *the Beloved is attempting to move her beyond the walls of the bedchamber to* **the next level** *of their relationship.* The intimacy is meant to draw her into Him, but it is not meant to wall her in and separate her from everything and everybody.

This is the wall of worship, intimacy, and surrender. It does serve a purpose to separate us from some of our distractions and draw us closer to the Beloved. Yet as wonderful as these things are, she is only halfway in her journey. She is ready for a new, *deeper* relationship with Him!

There must be a breaking down of the walls for there are *no walls* in the heavenly life toward which He beckons her. All divisions caused by sin *cease* in the new life.

> *"For it is a day of...treading down...by the Lord...in the valley of vision, breaking down the walls, and of crying to the mountains."* (Isaiah 22:5)

The Beloved is calling His bride to the heavenly life, where every wall must fall! All the divisions caused by sin must cease in this new life.

He calls her out from her cherished moments of intimate fellowship to catch His vision. It is time to *break down the walls* and *declare to the mountains* what is going on in her life.

Paul the apostle described how Jesus broke down the walls dividing us in Ephesians 2:14, "...He is our peace, who hath made both one, and hath *broken down* the middle wall of partition...."

Jesus described His goal as the Beloved nearly 1,000 years later in John's Gospel:

> *"I in them, and Thou in Me, that they may be made perfect in one; and that the world may know that Thou hast sent Me, and hast loved them, as Thou hast loved Me."* (John 17:23)

CHAPTER 8 – VULNERABLE

But look at her: The Soul in the "Banqueting House" (*Yayin*— House of wine ... worship ... intimacy) is not thinking of *others*, but is too absorbed in her gifts and delights.

The Soul in the banqueting house—whether it belongs to the Shulamite or to you or me—does not think about others. It is absorbed in her gifts and blessings.

Like Peter overawed on the Mount of transfiguration, the Soul would *forget* the multitude in the glory of the Transfiguration moment! She says, "Let's *build three tabernacles and stay here!*" (see (Matthew 17:4).

If she were being honest, she might say, "*Let the world die and go to hell. Let everybody else be ignored—just let me get blessed.*"

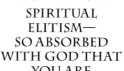

SPIRITUAL ELITISM— SO ABSORBED WITH GOD THAT YOU ARE UNCONCERNED WITH OTHERS.

That is spiritual elitism and I was like that at one time. We know we are infected when we become so absorbed with Him that we find it hard to concern ourselves with others.

If you have experienced these "Comforter joys," I'm sure you remember the temptation to focus exclusively on the Source of the joy while experiencing some *"elitist* spiritual self-esteem" during those blessed days?

Something is seriously wrong when we get so absorbed with Him that we don't want to concern ourselves with the "trifling" affairs of earth and *others*, or injustice around us, or "little foxes" within us.

"Our mother's sons (others in the Church) were incensed against us" because they saw our spiritual selfishness and feared lest the *vineyards* suffer (see Song of Solomon 1:6).

Later on, as she learns to "know Him" better, she will become "quick of scent" to His will, and will be able to *intuitively* detect his desires and movements.

Now she is too preoccupied with that which is happening to and within *her* to respond. She requires *plain* language—so plain language she's going to get.

THE CALL OF THE BELOVED

"My Beloved spake, and said unto me, Rise up, My friend, My fair one, and come away ... [For, lo (KJV)] The winter is past...the rain is over [and gone (KJV)] ... The flowers appear [on the earth (KJV)] ... the time of pruning [and the singing of birds (KJV)] is come ... Arise, My friend ... and come."
(Song of Solomon 2:10–13 ERV,
marginal notes, insertions mine)

The Shulamite woman has been redeemed. She has become a part of Him, the Body. She began by becoming His *friend* (*reyeh*), no longer hostile or merely an acquaintance.

She was more than that. She was submissive and surrendering, vulnerable and translucent. She was His *fair one* (*naveh*). When the Beloved calls her, He is not calling her *from* these positions of relationship, but *beyond* them!

The Soul knows His voice and that He speaks plainly to her.

The Shulamite hears Him say with insistent urgency...

"Rise up!"

Now, it was He who had wooed her to rest and brought her into the bedchambers. Then He said in Song of Solomon 2:7, "I charge you...daughters of Jerusalem...stir not up nor awake my love till she please."

CHAPTER 8 – VULNERABLE

Now He tells her, "Come away!" According to Keil and Delitzsch, the passage should read, "Go forth!"

Why? Where? What's going on? It is easy to get confused sometimes if you're not really sensitive to Him.

It was a shock to see Him appear outside of the wall, looking in through the lattice. She sees Him as a gazelle bouncing on the mountains. (I wonder if those mountains might include in our day the "seven mountains of influence" described by the late Bill Bright: religion, family, education, government, media, arts and entertainment, and business.)

Mountains always symbolize places of influence, places of power, and places of authority in the Scriptures. The Beloved is calling the Shulamite woman out of the bedchamber and into the world. He's calling her to her future and her destiny. He is calling her into servant-leadership.

She still doesn't understand, and the Beloved begins to speak plainly and directly in Song of Solomon 2:10-13 (quoted earlier).

The time has come when she must be taken deeper into identification with her Lord in His death and the subsequent resurrection life.

He senses that the Shulamite is able to move *forward*. The time has come when she must be taken deeper into identification with her Lord in His death and subsequent resurrection life.

Why? You can't serve God except from the resurrection life. He has to teach her what that means. He must draw her through Good Friday to get her to Easter Sunday. He must bring her through utter submission to get her to ultimate victory and glory.

So, He says, "Come away."

He died that He might bring us unto *God*.

Peter the apostle says, "Christ also hath once suffered . . . that He might *bring us to God* . . ." (1 Peter 3:18).

I also like the vivid description in Hebrews 10:20, "Through the rent veil of his flesh…" [*that's His crucifixion, isn't it?*], "…"By a new and living way which He hath consecrated for us through the veil, that is to say, His flesh…let us draw near."

The Beloved likens the past rest period to *winter* (Song of Solomon 2:11).

The Beloved is saying that *winter is the time to become rooted and grounded in God and in* **love**.

Paul's prayer for believers was "… that Christ may dwell in your hearts by faith; that ye, being rooted and grounded in *love*" (Ephesians 3:17–19).

If you can picture a husband cradling his wife's head and gently caressing her, then you have a picture of Christ [the Beloved] rooting and grounding His Bride in *love—agape* love.

This is how He teaches her His nature. Understand that I'm speaking *spiritually* when I say He is impregnating her with His character and essence.

Why? So that she "may be able to *comprehend* with all saints what is the breadth, and length, and depth, and height; and to know the love of Christ which passeth knowledge, that [she—the Church] might be *filled* with all of the fullness of God" (see Ephesians 3:17-19).

The Beloved calls her to rise up, because winter is past and spring is coming; the rain has come to prepare her for a new season.

CHAPTER 8 – VULNERABLE

Now the Shulamite has the benefits of a strong root system, and the Beloved knows that she is capable, prepared, and probably ready for Him to build an edifice of worship and ministry in her life that won't betray her or Him.

Remember, *spring is "resurrection" from the "death" of winter.*

In springtime, flowers appear in luxuriant growth sporting virtually every color in the rainbow, including vivid blues, greens, purples and reds. As gorgeous as it appears, the growth often begins to crowd in so much that it needs *pruning*.

Three key areas in every believer's life tend to exhibit exceptional growth during the winter of worship and need pruning and harnessing for the Beloved's use:

- **Knowledge**
- **New love**
- **New blessing**

The Beloved built up the Shulamite woman during the quiet time, enabling her to sink deep *roots* of love and worship into Him while in His presence.

Yet, even in the natural world, nature focuses on *root-growth* during the winter season to prepare for *blossoming* in spring.

Every skilled gardener and vintner knows that *root*-growth precedes and is required for *fruit*-growth! I like to think of worship as the winter of root-growth and spring as the time of fruit-growth.

You can't have the fruit without the root. The bigger the root: the more the fruit. The deeper the root: the sweeter and the more abundant the fruit.

THE MAKING OF A BRIDE

Now it is time for her to arise and learn to work *out* all that He has worked *in* her.

This is a new *kairos* time. *Kairos* is a Greek word meaning a "supreme or opportune moment, a season, a period of time with a definite characteristic."[1]

This is a new *kairos* season in her walk with Him! It is important to realize that He knows that she is ready—*even if she doesn't*.

Paul told us in Philippians 2:12b, "...Work out your *own* salvation with fear and trembling" (emphasis mine). Listen, you cannot follow the crowd in this—you must follow Him. While this pruning process takes place "in community," it is nevertheless deeply personal and totally volitional.

The new knowledge, love, and blessings need pruning and management for maximum fruitfulness in the coming season.

Now, that doesn't refer solely to wholesale cutting away and cutting back. A master vine keeper selectively *prunes or cuts away unfruitful "suckers."*

These unhealthy sprouts and misdirected growth pull away nutrients and life from the primary branches and block their access to the sun and rain necessary for maximum fruit.

PRUNING IS GOD'S WAY OF GETTING THE MOST FRUIT OUT OF YOUR LIFE.

Pruning is God's way to help you get the most fruit out of the new life that He gives you during your winter or worship season.

Now, remember where we find the Shulamite woman at the very end—He calls her a walled or a barred garden, full of fruit that He can invite the whole world to eat, knowing that she will produce more than enough. That is the "end game" and goal of the journey.

Paul the apostle reassured us with this promise in Philippians 1:6b (NKJV): "…He Who has begun a good work in you will *complete* it until the day of Jesus Christ."

The word translated as "complete" is *epiteleo*. It means "to accomplish, to bring to perfection, to consummate, to finish." Finally, look at the last six words: "…until the day of Jesus Christ."

Is that referring to "the end time"? No, it means the completion process will continue until this part of you is in communion and union with Him. It isn't complete until you can say of this stage, "It is finished."

Now we have arrived at the *center point* of "Soul's" journey. Here we discover the *key* to the Song of Solomon:

> *"O my dove, that art in the clefts of the rock,* **in the secret places of the stairs***, let Me see thy countenance, let Me hear thy voice; for sweet is thy voice, and thy countenance is comely."* (Song of Solomon 2:14, emphasis mine)

The key to our understanding of this book is the word, "stairs."

During a live lecture on this passage, one student asked me, "Where are you on these stair steps?" I said, "I believe that parts of me are on *nearly every step*."

The goal, of course, is to get all of us—and every part of our lives—on the twelfth step. Anything left on a lower step will impede our ability to go down the mountain in service and in ministry as the bride and representative of God in the earth.

That is the great metaphor and beautiful picture of The Song of Solomon.

THE MAKING OF A BRIDE

End Note – Separated (Vulnerable)

1. The Hebrew equivalent of *kairos* is *moed*.

STAGE C

LEGAL

FROM SECLUDED COMPANIONSHIP TO WEDDING PROCESSIONAL

The Seventh Stairstep – Secluded with Him
Chapter 9 – Betrothed (Chosen to Wed, Companion)
Chapter 10 – Betrothed (Valley of Trouble)

The Eighth Stairstep – Union with Him
Chapter 11 – Espoused (Legally Engaged)

The Ninth Stairstep – Transfigured by Him
Chapter 12 – Transported to the Wedding (Processional)

THE MAKING OF A BRIDE

CHAPTER 9

STAIRSTEP 7
SECLUDED WITH HIM

BETROTHED

(CHOSEN TO WED, COMPANION)

SONG OF SOLOMON 2:14-3:3

*"O my dove, that art in the clefts of the rock, in the **secret places of the stairs**, let Me see thy countenance, let Me hear thy voice; for sweet is thy voice, and thy countenance is comely."*
(Song of Solomon 2:14, emphasis mine)

THE CLEFT OF THE ROCK
BETROTHED & CHOSEN

Now the Shulamite woman has reached *Stairstep 7* in her journey with the King. This is a new, beautiful, and very decisive place for her because she becomes betrothed to the Beloved.

This is also where we find what I consider to be **the key to the whole book**, planted exactly in the middle of the 12 Steps. It appears in the 14th verse:

"O my dove, that art in *the clefts of the rock,* in the **secret places of the stairs...**"

THE MAKING OF A BRIDE

The King James Version and the 1881 Chicago Bible specifically include the phrase, "secret places of the stairs." Jessie Penn Lewis didn't quote the full verse in her exquisite book on the Song, *Thy Hidden Ones*, perhaps because the idea of the stair steps wasn't in her thinking.

Remember that when the verse begins with, "Oh My dove," it is the Beloved speaking to the Shulamite. He goes on to say, "... that art in *the clefts of the rock*."

He already sees her where He *wants* her to be, even though she isn't there presently. And yet, in a real sense, she went into "the clefts of the rock" the day she was saved (understand that I am using a metaphor here).

You see, Christ Jesus is the Rock and the "cleft of the rock" is His cross, where He received the incision. What did the Roman soldier find when he pushed his spear under Jesus' fifth rib and pierced His heart? The Bible says, "But one of the soldiers with a spear pierced His side, and forthwith came there out *blood and water*" (John 19:34, emphasis mine).

This is the picture of the cleft of the rock, the pierced heart and body of Jesus. From it flows the blood of redemption and the water of the Holy Spirit, symbolic of our new life in Christ.

Then the Beloved continues:

> "... that art ... **in the secret places of the stairs,** let Me see thy countenance, let Me hear thy voice; for sweet is thy voice, and thy countenance is comely."
> (Song of Solomon 2:14, emphasis mine)

The Hebrew word translated as "secret" is *cethar*, a word that also means "hiding place." This particular word isn't used to say

CHAPTER 9 – BETROTHED (CHOSEN TO WED)

that something is "secret" as a mystery. It speaks more of a secret place that is cramped and difficult to get to, a place where not everyone can thrive.

The late Corrie ten Boom wrote a great biographical book entitled, *The Hiding Place*. This is the Bible passage that inspired her title. It was in the *hiding place*, the *cethar*, that she treasured all of the little ones she and her family were hiding from the Nazis. Her family home became a *cethar*, a secret hiding place.

The Hebrew word translated as "the stairs" is *madregah*. The scholars Keil and Delitzsch translate it literally as "stair rocks." It means stair steps, or an inaccessible place.

Picture an incision, a hole or step carved into the rock. Anyone hidden in that rock step is *safe*.

The Song of Solomon is a divine picture of how we begin to grow by walking up the stair steps, the *madregah*, in the clefts in The Rock—Christ.

The Cross is everywhere in Scripture.

Again, it is here at *Stairstep 7* that the Shulamite woman—a picture of you and me—becomes betrothed to the Beloved (a picture of the Resurrected Christ) through the Cross.

The picture of what happened on the Cross appears generations earlier in the Book of Exodus under the ministry of Moses:

> "Behold, I will stand before thee there upon the rock in Horeb; and thou shalt smite the **rock**, and there shall come water out of it, that the people may drink. And Moses did so in the sight of the elders of Israel." (Exodus 17:6, emphasis mine)

THE MAKING OF A BRIDE

This is an early picture of how Jesus was *smitten* by God for us. We also see His suffering and crucifixion foretold vividly by Isaiah the prophet about 700 years before the Lord's birth:

> *"Surely He hath borne our griefs, and carried our sorrows: yet we did esteem Him **stricken, smitten** of God, and afflicted.*
>
> *"But He was wounded for our transgressions, He was bruised for our iniquities: the chastisement of our peace was upon Him; and with His stripes we are healed."*
> (Isaiah 53:4-5, emphasis mine)

An especially vivid picture of "the cleft in the rock" appears in God's statement to Moses who asked to *see* God. This brief sentence contains the entire picture!

> *"And it shall come to pass, while My glory passeth by, that I will put thee **in a clift [cleft] of the rock**, and will cover thee with My hand while I pass by."* (Exodus 33:22, emphasis mine)

This is the biblical imagery that the people in the court of Solomon are drawing from. I am convinced that Solomon wrote the Song in consultation with wise men who peopled his court, men who had treasured the traditions of Israel in their spirit for years upon years, and generations upon generations.

> *"O my dove, that art in **the clefts of the rock,** in the **secret places of the stairs,** let Me see thy countenance, let Me hear thy voice; for sweet is thy voice, and thy countenance is comely."* (Song of Solomon 2:14, emphasis mine)

These are the words of the Beloved speaking to His redeemed one, whose eyes He seeks to turn toward Calvary.

Why would he do that? He *turns us toward Calvary because it is only there that He can bring us to **glory**.*

CHAPTER 9 – BETROTHED (CHOSEN TO WED)

This may shock you, but I don't believe that God wants us to always live "in the shadow" of the Cross. Not in every sense of that phrase. I think He wants us to live in the joy of the dawning of the new kingdom.

> GOD WANTS US TO LIVE IN THE JOY OF THE DAWNING OF THE NEW KINGDOM.

The only problem is that you can't get to the glory except through the Cross. *He must take us to the Cross to take us to glory.* We must go through suffering in order to reach joy unspeakable and full of glory.

The Apostle Paul understood this. He said, "For if we have been planted together in the likeness of His death, we shall be also in the likeness of His resurrection" (Romans 6:5).

There can be no *"resurrected life"* apart from a *"crucified one."*

This passage in Song of Solomon 2:14 is a picture of the Beloved Savior *teaching His Bride that she is hidden in His wounded side, planted by the Holy Spirit into His death.*

The cleft of the rock is His *wounded* side. (The Hebrew word translated as "cleft" is *hagah*. It refers to "a slit, a cut, a place of concealment, a refuge.")

Remember Isaiah's prophetic picture of Jesus the Messiah: "But He was wounded [*pierced through*] for our transgressions..." (Isaiah 53:5a, emphasis and insertion mine).

To this point, the Shulamite woman has known Him as her Indwelling King, but she has not come to understand her position as *"buried with Him* into His *death,"* and therefore separated from her old self and her old life.

This is the "Romans Six Life." I love the Book of Romans and Romans Chapter 6 in particular, because it describes what I call "The Crucified Life."

(The Crucified Life is so important to our understanding of who we are in Christ that I invited Dr. Sam Drye, of Macon, Georgia, to develop and teach a Bible college course by that title. I encourage you to prayerfully read Romans 6:1-14, especially verses 3-6 to help you grasp this vital truth.)

The Beloved reminds her of her place in "The Cleft of the Rock"; here she is His *betrothed*.

Up until this point, they were only courting.

Remember that we have twelve great steps in our journey to maturity in Christ. The fourth step marks the place where she comes into relationship with Him. She goes through Steps 5 and 6 before she is finally betrothed to Him in this seventh step.

When I say she was "betrothed," I'm saying that she was *promised* to Him from that moment forward. It was and is still common in portions of the Middle East for families of a prospective couple to get together and formally decide that the marriage will take place.

The "marriage" isn't legally binding yet; in fact it's not even a legal *engagement* at this point. It is a betrothing, a promising. For instance, Mary was betrothed or *promised* to Joseph at an early age.

The Shulamite woman becomes espoused to the Beloved in the next stage or great turning point, and there is a difference between betrothal and espousement.

CHAPTER 9 – BETROTHED (CHOSEN TO WED)

A *betrothal* was a spoken agreement between two families concerning future plans for their children to marry. When two people were publicly *espoused*, it was a legally binding commitment that was so serious that it took a divorce to break the vows.

Remember that even before they were formally married, Joseph considered "putting away" Mary privately—or quietly *divorcing* her—because of her unexplained pregnancy. It took angelic intervention to preserve their epousement and future marriage (see Matthew 1:19-20).

Where does this promising, this state of "chosen-ness" leading to betrothal take place?

The Beloved and the Shulamite woman became exclusive with one another as they continued courting and getting acquainted. Then He chose her and nobody else at this seventh stage.

How can He do that? Why?

It is now, in the Cleft of the Rock, that they become "legally engaged!" She is in Him and she is His.

This is the mid-point of their relationship; now they can proceed to become one. This is a picture of her coming into union and fellowship in His death. There is a lot involved in this process and it covers three or four steps.

The bride for the first Adam was taken out of his side as he slept, made of Adam's own nature and presented to him by the Creator. Eve is a perfect foreshadow of the Church and her Lord, the Christ.

> "And the Lord took one of his ribs ... and ... made ... a woman ... and they ... one flesh."　　　　　　(Genesis 2:21-24)

THE MAKING OF A BRIDE

All of the redeemed, born of the first Adam and under the curse, were, in the foreknowledge of God, planted into the God-man, the *second* Adam, who hung on the Cross and became a curse for them.

Now, this is what is being pictured here when she was *placed "in the cleft of the rock"* and covered with His hand (His *authority*).

Paul saw that when he said, *"We thus judge that One died for all, therefore all died"* (2 Corinthians 5:14).

The full story is formed in the metaphor of the wilderness journey that begins here. This next great division also marks *the key moment for Sister Soul* because this is when she becomes legally His. It is here that she moves out of *experiences* and into *relationship*. This is incredibly wonderful progress.

This next statement is *the heart and soul of Jessie Penn-Lewis' book, Thy Hidden Ones*. She doesn't take into account the stair steps that are so clear and dear to me, but I agree with her insights on Song of Solomon 2:14:

*"We who are planted in Him, baptized into His death, shall emerge as His **Bride**, formed of many members, taken out of His side in the sleep of death, partaking of His divine nature, and eventually we shall be presented unto Him to share His throne"* (Jessie Penn-Lewis, p. 54).

That is the heart of the revelation of the Song of Solomon and its central theme according to Jesse Penn-Lewis.

The Beloved invites her to turn her face toward Him and respond to His call.

She wants to stay in the worship chamber. There is a problem here that afflicts many Christians at this point in their spiritual journey with Jesus:

CHAPTER 9 – BETROTHED (CHOSEN TO WED)

He sees that she is focused in the *wrong* direction!

The problem is that she is focused on *uninterrupted worship*. There is a good chance that you weren't alive yet when the charismatic movement or experience first started.

I was there. We all broke off into cell groups and Bible studies—which isn't a bad thing, but unfortunately we were so inwardly focused that we didn't care about anything or anybody else.

We collected audio-cassette teaching tapes on every verse in the Bible (we don't use them anymore, but they were cutting edge in the late 1970s and 1980s). We proudly carried our big Bibles, our little Bibles, our old masking-taped Bibles, and our brand new Bibles to meetings and in public—but we were too inner-focused.

That's where the Shulamite is at this point. *She still looks **within** for His manifested presence*, looking for any sign of a personal blessing or revelation.

*The problem is that the Beloved now wants her to turn toward Him, not in **intimacy** and **worship** but as "in His Father's bosom."*

What do I mean by that?

He longs for her to turn to Him as a sunflower turns to the sun, or as the moon to the sun, without emotional or physical *reward* in mind.

Who has to call a meeting or ring a bell or announce the dawn for a sunflower to turn toward the sun? No one. It's nature. It's natural.

He wants to become everything to her. He wants her to turn toward *Him*—not merely *His*—not even His blessing, His provision, or His worship. *Him.*

THE MAKING OF A BRIDE

*This is union—**oneness** with Him.* It is more than a supernatural experience or even a remarkable commitment. This is *union*, and thus is deeper than all of these other things combined. This is oneness with Him.

It means becoming one with Him:

- *Not for what we feel* – although the feeling is wonderful.
- *Not for what we get.* The revelation is absolutely magnificent. The gifts are supreme. "I've lived many a year," David said, "and never seen God's children begging bread."
- *Not for what we learn, but for Him.*

THE SOUL'S PREOCCUPIED REPLY

Look at where the Shulamite woman is—her response to the Beloved's call is staggering to me. This may well be the **greatest verse in the book!**

> "Take us the foxes, the little foxes that spoil the vines ... My Beloved is mine, and I am His; He feedeth ... among the lilies."
> (Song of Solomon 2:15–16)

This passage in its context would have been nonsensical to me if I hadn't found the key to the Song of Solomon, but it isn't. It is an appropriate expression of where she is.

She hears His voice.

Many times in the Song the Bible says of the Shulamite, "She hears his voice." She always knows her Beloved's voice.

Again, this is a key difference between the bride and the virgins. Sometimes the virgins don't know His voice. Remember that Jesus said, "My sheep hear my voice, and I know them, and they follow me" (John 10:27).

CHAPTER 9 – BETROTHED (CHOSEN TO WED)

The Shulamite knew His voice, every time she heard it. Even if she was confused by what He said or asked, as is the case here. Understand that this is the heart of the Book of Song of Solomon.

She hears His message about the Cross but she does not understand.

We need to pay attention at this point. Why? If you ask 99 percent of the body of Christ today, *"What could be better than worship, blessing, submission?"* They'll say, "Nothing."

She is preoccupied with her *vineyard*, to be more excellent in her *perfection* for Him.

How many of us have thought along those same lines, *When it comes to our spiritual relationship with Him, what could be better than anointing and ministry and holiness?*

Now I am assuming that since we have already covered some of this in previous chapters, that you wouldn't say what most folks would say: "Nothing."

Unfortunately, I suspect that most of the body of Christ would say, "Nothing is better than anointing, ministry, and holiness. That's where it is at. That is what it's all about."

Yet the King says, "No, those things are a part of our relationship. But there's something more, something even deeper, something even better."

In the King's chambers, she had learned that she had been too much engrossed in her ministry and had neglected her own vineyard (her personal union with Him).

Now she goes to the other extreme and is so occupied with her own *holiness* as to be unable to hear His call.

THE MAKING OF A BRIDE

Isn't that an incredible statement?

"How could that possibly be? That sounds like nonsense."

In Acts 10, we learn that God was about to do something brand new in Peter's life and in His Kingdom on earth. He was about to take the gospel from Judaism into the wider non-Jewish world.

He let the disciple see a vision in which a sheet was lowered to the roof containing all kinds of ceremonially unclean animals which the Jewish people were forbidden to eat under the Law of Moses.

Then the Lord said, "Rise, Peter. Kill and eat."

> *"But Peter said, Not so, Lord; for I have never eaten any thing that is common [koinos - unholy] or unclean [akathartos - impure]."* (Acts 10:14, insertions mine)

God had something **new** for Peter, but he almost missed it. He was saying, basically, "Not me, Lord! That's against my religion." Once Peter "got it," *God used him to open the Gospel to the Gentile world!*

That is exactly where the Shulamite woman is at the point where the Beloved calls her out of the intimate chambers. Her religion was in His gifts, His blessings, her holiness and her ministry—not necessarily in Him.

One of the reasons Evangelist Jim Bakker managed to recover after his great fall from internationally known TV evangelist to Federal prison inmate was that *he realized his error* while in prison.

Bakker later said, "The reason that I fell is that I made my ministry my God. PTL ['Praise The Lord' television network] took God's place. And I thought as long as I was working at PTL, then that was all I needed. I didn't need God." This is a picture of what "work and no worship" produces.

CHAPTER 9 – BETROTHED (CHOSEN TO WED)

Little foxes are manifestations of the *old* life.

These "foxes" are destroyers of excellence and perfection. They represent the carnal life, a life dominated by the flesh.

They ruin the harvest before it is gathered. They spoil the vines of ministry, worship, and personal correctness.

The Shulamite woman missed this truth at this point and said, "Take the little foxes, Lord. I'll be better. I'll be better in my worship. I'll get better in my ministry. I'll study harder. I'll pray more. But don't take me out of worship, relationship, intimacy with you."

She didn't understand that she was substituting these wonderful things—ministry, worship, gifts, and blessings—for Him, and choosing them over Him.

Meanwhile, He was trying to draw her into a higher and even better way.

"If her eyes had been on *Him* and not *herself*—even her successes—she would have risen up and *He* would have taken care of the foxes." (Jesse Penn-Lewis)

Obedience is better than sacrifice.

Let me give you a "refrigerator statement" that I learned many years ago in seminary. I really didn't know it before then.

I didn't go to seminary right out of college or high school. I finally went into seminary in the middle of a seven-year stint as the pastor of a local church. This is what I learned:

It is so much better to be *"with God"* than it is to be *"good."*

No one should mistake this statement as a license to be bad because that really isn't the issue. *If you are with God, then **He** defines* *what is good* based on the eternal principles of heaven rather than the often warped principles of earth.

*The Shulamite wanted to **serve better, worship better,** and **be holier.*** He said, "No, no, no, darling. I just want YOU, not your performance!"

We must flee to the cleft of the rock and hide in Him.

When we do, *He* **will take care of the foxes.**

You and I aren't equipped to deal with "foxes" in our lives anyway. We can't handle foxes. In fact, we can't even catch them. So, how are we supposed to deal with them?

The "spoilers of the vine" in our lives—our failures and our imperfections—*become* **His responsibility** if we stay in the Cleft of the Rock.

Neither our holiness or our ministry is up to us – He must make them both successful.

I wish I had learned this lesson years and years ago. For a period in my life I was just another play soldier in the ministry, keeping rules and regulations without depth of relationship with God.

Listen, it is impossible to keep religious rules and regulations perfectly without relationship. We can only do it when we allow it to become His responsibility while we hide in Him.

Chapter 10

STAIRSTEP 7 – CONTINUED
BETROTHED
(THE VALLEY OF TROUBLE)

*"**My beloved** is mine, and I am **His**: He feedeth among the lilies.*

*"Until the day break, and the shadows flee away, **turn, my beloved,** and be Thou like a roe or a young hart upon the mountains of Bether."*
(Song of Solomon 2:16-17, italic emphasis mine)

What a wonderful declaration: "My beloved is mine, and I am His…." It is true.

However, the Shulamite is avoiding the Beloved's call when she says this! She turns her attention on the place she wants *Him* to go rather than where He is calling her. And this brings her to the Valley of Trouble.

Surely not! We must be reading this passage incorrectly.

Notice that it is the Shulamite who begins the passage with, "My Beloved." Then consider what she says: "Until the day break, and the shadows flee away, *turn, my Beloved,* and be thou like a gazelle on the mountains of separation."

Do you know what she is doing here?

THE MAKING OF A BRIDE

Because she failed to understand His call to arise and follow Him, He hid His face from her.

She is saying, "Come back, come back." It may not be clear to you yet, but it will dawn on you in just a minute.

He asked her to turn toward Him and she responded by talking about *vineyards* and *foxes*.

In Song of Solomon 2:10, the Shulamite says, "*My beloved* spoke and said to me, 'Arise, my darling/my beautiful one, come with me'" (italic emphasis mine).

In verses 13 and 14, the Beloved continues His call to the Shulamite:

"**Arise**, come, my darling;
my beautiful one, **come with me**.
"My dove in the clefts of the rock,
in the hiding places on the mountainside,
"show Me your face,
let Me hear your voice;
"for your voice is sweet,
and your face is lovely."
(Song of Solomon 2:13b-14, italic emphasis mine).

He is calling her to join Him in ministry despite her imperfections. She focuses on busyness and unworthiness, and tries to compel Him to remain hidden away from His calling to stay with her.

He is saying repeatedly in various ways, "Come away. Come away with me to a wilderness."

CHAPTER 10 – BETROTHED (VALLEY OF TROUBLE)

She had been in the banqueting house and in the chambers of intimate fellowship. She'd been enjoying His gifts and His caresses, and she was feeling wonderful.

The problem was that it was *so* good that she didn't want to go anywhere or do anything for anyone. I understand that. Charismatic spiritual Christians may well understand that better than anyone else does.

After all, what could be better than feeling good in God's presence? We spend most of our time in our churches trying to make them centers for worship, joy, blessing, anointing.

"Oh, didn't we have great church service?" Yes, we did. But were we equipped to do something? Did we get equipped to leap like gazelles over and above the seven mountains of influence in the world to change lives in His name?

Jesus knew far more than we do about the wonders of lingering in the glory and wonder of God's throne room, but *something compelled Him* to leave His heavenly glory behind and step into our fallen world to lay down His life for us—while we "were yet sinners" (see Romans 5:8).

Today He calls us to *do the same.*

We are called to win the world and see His kingdom come on earth. The Bible says, *"The kingdoms* of this world are become *the kingdoms of our Lord, and of his Christ; and* he shall reign for ever and ever" (Revelation 11:15b).

WE ARE CALLED TO WIN THE WORLD AND SEE HIS KINGDOM COME ON EARTH.

That is our job.

The Beloved is getting the Shulamite ready to help him do the work of the Kingdom. He's calling her beyond comfort and even the blessings of intimacy with Him. He knows she has the goods and her roots are deep enough now. So He is calling her to her destiny.

Unfortunately, she did what we often do. She was saying in essence, "Lord, don't make me go. Come back. I'll worship better. I'll pray better. I'll give more."

She doesn't get it yet.

When He told her about the hiding place in the Cleft of the Rock, she sank back upon her old experience and said, "My Beloved is mine" (see Song of Solomon 2:16).

"Look, look at how I can worship. I love to worship You. I praise, I dance, I weep, and I even prophesy. I *know* how to worship You!"

"Just look at all of the blessings You've given me. After all, I am an intercessor and a worshipper. Look at all of the things I do here…do we have to leave?"

She cannot yet fellowship with Him in the fellowship of His *sufferings*.

This is the realm of the mature. She can't go there yet; it is out of her "comfort zone."

This is beyond the "doing level" of her relationship.

At this level, there is no more "performance." It is being. Indeed, it is dying.

So, the Beloved hides Himself to see what *silence* will do.

Let me give you another "refrigerator" statement: *"Yesterday's manna will not suffice for today."* Yesterday's revelation can become "putrid bread" unsuitable for today's anointing and calling.

CHAPTER 10 – BETROTHED (VALLEY OF TROUBLE)

Had she been sensitive to His leading, He would not have needed to *withdraw*. (Jesse Penn-Lewis)

Here is another refrigerator statement: *"God will not take you where you **refuse** to go."* Be careful in the way you respond when God speaks.

If we would leave ourselves totally in His hands and without self-centeredness, how quickly He could take us in to *dwell* in the secret place of the Most High!

If we let go and totally trust Him, He will enable us to walk straight up these twelve stairsteps and right into bridehood, mature service and love.

He wants us to *live habitually* and *make our home* in the secret place of the Most High.

His silence arrests her self-absorption.

Oddly enough, *this is to her credit.* Why? I say it again; *her hunger for Him is her greatest attribute.* This is what separates the bride from the virgins.

Most church folks aren't hungry after God so much as they hunger for His blessings and anointing. They say, *"I want to get a blessing today. I want something wonderful to happen today."*

"I hear you, but what about Him?"

The Shulamite woman is now *aware of a cloud between them*. She seems to sense *distance and confusion*, and she feels *dry and cold*. It is as if she were saying, *"My religion is not working."*

Have you ever been in this place?

I don't have enough hands, feet, toes and fingers to raise for that question! I've been in that place far too many times. God was actually trying to take me to a new place, a new depth or a new height in Him, but *I didn't want to go because I didn't understand it.*

Most of us expect "the way we've always done it" to always "do it." We want our old ways to carry us all the way. Jesus doesn't see it that way. Remember, it was *Jesus* who said:

> *"No one puts new wine into old wineskins; otherwise the wine will burst the skins, and the wine is lost and the skins as well; but **one puts new wine into fresh wineskins**."*
> (Mark 2:21-22, emphasis mine)

We must be able to accommodate the new things of God into the old things and old ways we've already learned.

*The Shulamite woman is still in the dawn of her relationship with Him but she is moving toward the time when she can truly be **one** with Him.*

This is progress, but it is painful progress!

She is moving toward but has not yet reached that day, which will be "... as the light of the morning, when the sun riseth, even a morning without clouds" (see 2 Samuel 23:4).

She *calls out* to Him from the shadows of *separation* (bether – a Hebrew term for separation).

Look at her amazing statement:

> *"**Until the day break, and the shadows flee away, turn, my Beloved, and be Thou like a gazelle ... upon the mountains of separation (bether)**."*
> (Song of Solomon 2:17, ERV, marginal notes)

This statement was birthed in the worship chamber when the Beloved suddenly appeared *outside* of the chamber as a gazelle, bounding on the seven mountains of influence.

CHAPTER 10 – BETROTHED (VALLEY OF TROUBLE)

He calls her out of the chamber to join Him in the wilderness, but she says, "Lord, turn around. Stop what You are doing and come back to me."

*She is instructing **Him** now! She is saying, "Come back to me on **my terms**! Forget **Your purpose** and return to **my presence**. Don't You understand? My religion must work!"*

I've forgotten how many times I have done the same thing and ruined my possibilities in those moments! Each time I literally curbed and delayed my development in God.

Does He answer that cry? No!

The Beloved doesn't answer that cry. As the prophet Zephaniah says, *"The Lord is **silent** in His love"* (Zephaniah 3:17).

Now He is gone and she will not follow.

*This is her greatest single test: "The **silence** of God."*

If you have never experienced this, let me give you some bad news and some good news. The bad news is that if you are worth anything in the Kingdom, then you *will* experience His divine silence.

The good news is that "the silence of God" is actually a door to your future.

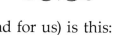

THE "SILENCE OF GOD" IS A DOOR TO YOUR FUTURE.

The important question for the Shulamite (and for us) is this: *Will she be able to move from 'doing' to 'being' in the relationship?* The greatest tragedy of all would have been if she had not continued to hunger after Him.

Sadly, many millions of believers have stopped right at this point, the point that takes them toward bridehood.

The truth is that He is getting her ready for the very next stage: legal engagement.

THE SEEKING SOUL AND HER DECISION

"By night on my bed I sought Him...but I found Him not. I will rise now...I will seek Him ..." (Song of Solomon 3:1-2)

I don't know how long this impasse of the wills went on. For some, it takes a matter of days or weeks. Others suffer in stubbornness for months, while a few agonize in isolation for decades. It takes *an act of the **will** to experience the exhilaration of this major breakthrough.*

She's now in the darkness of night. She sought Him in the intimacy (bed) of *worship* **and found Him not.**

Where did God go? Many books and sermons have focused on the absence of God. I've preached on it myself. The Shulamite is about to learn a life-lesson that benefits us all.

She finally reaches the place where she says, "I will rise now and I will seek Him."

Here is another great statement:

> Sometimes, God must turn yesterday's bread
> into stone to move us forward.
> Sometimes, He must dry up the Brook Cherith
> before we will go on to Zarephath!

Had the Beloved not been absent from all of the places where the Shulamite had found him earlier, she would never have gone to the *new place* with Him.

She didn't realize that He had already built the next fire (like the great teacher I mentioned who so impacted my life). He had

CHAPTER 10 – BETROTHED (VALLEY OF TROUBLE)

already gone on before her to lay the path that would take her to a new level.

Now it was time to pour some water on this fire and move on to the next and better fire.

In desolation, she rises up to seek Him in activity or wherever He may be found.

This is to her great credit; it is a great credit to us as well if we, too, rise up to seek Him in moments of darkness.

> *"Behold, I go forward, but He is not there...backward, but I cannot perceive Him.*
>
> *"On the left hand...but I cannot behold Him...He hideth Himself on the right hand, that I cannot see Him ...*
>
> *"God hath made my heart faint...but I am not dismayed because of the darkness"*
>
> *"... nor because thick darkness covers my face"*
> (Job 23:8-9, 16-17—ERV, marginal notes)

Job had come to the same place the Shulamite would find herself—facing the silence of God. He declared his decision even before he encountered his greatest silence from God: *"Though He slay me, yet will I trust in Him"* (Job 13:15a).

Job's response is echoed in the words of poet Robert Louis Stevenson who wrote many millennia later, "I believe in God. And if I died and woke up in hell tomorrow, I would still believe in God."

Job wanted God. The Shulamite wanted God. She would do whatever it took to have Him. If it meant leaving the blessing, if it meant leaving the place of intimacy, if it meant *leaving everything else and everybody else*, she was going to go after Him!

THE MAKING OF A BRIDE

This reminds us of one of the "hardest" sayings of Jesus' ministry when He tried to communicate to His followers the level of commitment in true discipleship:

> *"If any man come to Me, and hate not his father, and mother, and wife, and children, and brethren, and sisters, yea, and his own life also, he cannot be My disciple."* (Luke 14:26)

This is the Shulamite's greatest moment and her hardest. While I can't speak about your experience, I know that I've been there.

The good news is that if you have a hunger for God and you want God in your life at whatever cost, you are the bride. None of us is perfect in this life, but we must know in our hearts that our number one priority in life is that we may know *Him*.

You and I may not be all the way up the staircase of discipleship in every area or dimension of our lives, but we have "bride" written all over us. Now God can use us.

> *"By night on my bed I sought Him…but I found Him not. I will rise now…I will seek Him …"* (Song of Solomon 3:1-2)

Perhaps the Shulamite got a little angry and frustrated. Maybe she'd just had enough of the waiting in silence.

> *"I will rise now and I will seek Him, wherever He can be found."*

She's in the darkness of night. She had sought Him in worship, the intimacy of worship, the bed of worship. In desolation, she finally rises to seek Him, wherever she must—even through the seemingly illogical call into the wilderness. She will do whatever she must.

CHAPTER 10 – BETROTHED (VALLEY OF TROUBLE)

If you're worth anything at all to the Kingdom, there will be a time in your life when you will come here as well. Seriously, this is the way through to who you are and what God's called you to do and be.

She is not dismayed because of the separation, but she determines that she's going to seek Him with her whole heart.

This is a great moment for Sister Soul. In fact, it is perhaps the greatest moment. *Many lose heart at this stage and don't go forward.*

Now she's focused on *Him*; *not* her *experiences* in Him, *nor* her *ministry* for Him, *nor* her *gifts* from Him, *nor* her *holiness* before Him.

All of these things are wonderful.

However, *when they are chosen instead of Him, they become the enemy.*

How can holiness, ministry, or worship be an enemy? **Only** when they *take His place* in our lives. Once again, *these are His but they are not **Him**.*

She doesn't care who knows about her desperation as long as she finds Him.

By this stage, the Shulamite woman is transparent, not self-centered.

Most folks would try to go through this struggle quietly and without anybody knowing what is going on. This woman is so desperate for Him that she doesn't care who knows that she's not perfect!

She is so desperate for Him that she doesn't care who knows that she doesn't "have it all together." It doesn't matter that the secret slipped out that she isn't some super person or super saint. *He alone is **central** to her.*

The Beloved has succeeded in His purpose.

His silence has done what His presence could not. *He called her to arise and she didn't obey. It was by hiding His face from her that He drew her into His will and into His purpose.*

He allowed her to look for Him in all the *old* places where she had been with Him before.

God has done that with me on several occasions, I'm sad to say. In each case, it was because I just couldn't grasp God's purpose in any other way. My mind would recite the usual litany of "logical" excuses: *Why should I change? Look, I'm so successful in doing His business. I'm so happy and blessed, and everything is going my way. Why should I change now?*

The Beloved remained hidden from her, and in His absence she experienced dryness and coldness. She discovered that *He didn't seem to be present in the old blessings, the old successes, and the old manna.* He didn't seem present because *He had something **new** for her: a new, deeper place in Him.*

Lamentations 3:33 says, "He doth not afflict willingly nor grieve the children of men."

Paul the apostle declared in Romans 8:28: *"And we know that all things work together for good to them that love God, to them who are the called according to His purpose"* (KJV).

Whenever it seems that God is absent for no real reason, understand that He has something new, something better for you if you will just continue to follow *Him!*

CHAPTER 10 – BETROTHED (VALLEY OF TROUBLE)

He has already gone ahead of you to "build a new fire." The one warming your life to this point has served its purpose. Now you're outgrowing it and Jesus has moved to a higher place.

GOD HAS SOMETHING BETTER FOR YOU ... JUST FOLLOW HIM!

You will never experience the wonder of the new things He has for you tomorrow if nothing manages to help you move *beyond* where you are right now.

Joyfully, the Beloved watches her rise and obey Him and seek *Him* above all.

The discouraged disciples in the first century faced moments of decision again and again after Jesus' resurrection, each time being called or pressed by circumstances to rise up and seek out, call out, or move out to seek Jesus.

It happened in the middle of a fierce storm on the Sea of Galilee in the Gospel of Mark:

> *"And He saw them toiling in rowing; for the wind was contrary unto them: and about the fourth watch of the night He cometh unto them, walking upon the sea, and would have passed by them.*
>
> *"But when **they saw Him walking** upon the sea, they supposed it had been a spirit, and **cried out**."*
>
> Mark 6:48-49, emphasis mine)

It also happened to two disheartened disciples walking along the Emmaus Road in Luke 24:

> *"And they drew nigh unto the village, whither they went: and He made as though He would have gone further.*

THE MAKING OF A BRIDE

*"But **they constrained Him**, saying, **Abide with us** ..."*
(Luke 24:28-29, emphasis mine)

By the time their encounter with the Risen Lord was completed, they were burning with zeal and determined to convince others that Jesus was risen indeed and full of power.

There is always a reward for those who *seek Him*.

CHAPTER 11

STAIRSTEP 8
UNION WITH HIM
ESPOUSED (LEGALLY ENGAGED)

SONG OF SOLOMON 3:4-5

*"It was but a little that I passed from **them**, but I found Him whom my soul loveth: I held Him, and would not let Him go, until I had brought Him into my mother's house, and into the chamber of her that conceived me.*

"I charge you, O ye daughters of Jerusalem, by the roes, and by the hinds of the field, that ye stir not up, nor awake my love, till He please."   (Song of Solomon 3:4-5, emphasis mine)

How small a step sometimes stands between the soul and victory!

We opened *Stairstep 8* of the Stairs with Song of Solomon 3:4, "It was but a little that I passed from *them*, when I found Him...I held Him, and would not let Him go" (emphasis mine).

What or who is *"them"* in this passage?

Well, it represents the virgins, to be sure. However, it may also include all of the old blessings, all of the old manna, all of the old "stuff" that had brought her to where she was. Now this was "good stuff," not bad. No one should criticize any of that.

However, notice that she said, "*When I passed* from **them**, I *found Him*."

He was there all the time. He had never really gone anywhere. He was just calling her to a higher plane.

How small a step sometimes stands between the soul and victory!

Now here is another great statement:

"He is always in the right place. It is I who sometimes moves away."

It's not answers to my questions, not blessings, not ministry that I need. **It is to go where He is.** *From there all of those other things will flow out of me so profusely and so profoundly that everybody will know that I have been with Him.*

I am reminded of the remarkable statement those who crucified Jesus made about Peter and John:

> "Now when they saw the boldness of Peter and John, and perceived that they were unlearned and ignorant men, they marveled; and they took knowledge of them, that **they had been with Jesus.**" (Acts 4:13, emphasis mine)

So I don't need to seek those things. I just need to seek Him. All of those things I need are *in Him*.

We must come to desperation and throw ourselves totally upon God!

That outer wall (you remember when the Shulamite said, "He was on the outside of our wall"?) *has got to come down!*

CHAPTER 11 – ESPOUSED (LEGALLY ENGAGED)

That wall covers our failures and maintains our "self-image" or "reputation." Let it fall! If Jesus "made himself of no *reputation, and took upon him the form of a servant*" (see Philippians 2:7), then why should we prop up our reputations?

Only when everything else failed did she cry out for Him with no self-concerns.

The Shulamite woman is a thoroughly human representative of the Bride of Christ. Like so many us, she only turned to Him *when everything else failed*!

She "passed from them"—all self-interest; self-glory; self-complacency; and self-appropriation.

Her yearning for Him created a *vacuum* ready for God to fill.

Most of us have heard this often-quoted line, *"Inside every man there is a God-shaped vacuum, and all of life is empty until that vacuum is filled."*

It was probably inspired by the writings of St. Augustine[1] and later on by the French philosopher and mathematician, Pascal.[2] Regardless of the source of the quote, its content very accurately describes our universal longing for God.

Paul declared, "For it is God which worketh in you, both to will and to do of His good pleasure" (Philippians 2:13).

When we say the Shulamite's yearning created *"a vacuum ready for God to fill,"* we also say "that's what God does." He makes us hungry for Him and then He comes and fills that hunger.

"I found Him."

The key to being a bride (instead of merely a virgin) is *to hunger for Him*.

When her hunger for Him overcomes her fears and personal desires for other things, finally she says, *"I found Him!"*

Nothing else worked but, oh, "I found Him."

What joy this is for her!

What a joy it is to find Him after waiting and wandering in our own plans.

But even here she does not quite understand Him. Not yet....

Despite her progress, even after finally reuniting with her Beloved after an agonizing separation, the Shulamite doesn't quite get it. She says, *"I held Him and would not let Him go."*

His *"manifested presence"* is so precious that she clings to it and *"will not let Him go."*

Even here, *she is still trying to squeeze or press Him into her mold.* Old paradigms die hard!

Perhaps that is why Jesus solemnly warned His disciples, "And no man putteth new wine into old bottles: else the new wine doth burst the bottles, and the wine is spilled, and the bottles will be marred: but new wine must be put into new bottles" (Mark 2:22).

She tries to press this new dimension of her relationship with her Beloved into her old mold of *worship, possession,* and *control.* Many young brides battle insecurity in their early weeks and months of marriage, and jealously press their new husbands to stay by their side despite the natural need to work jobs, attend church, and tend to the basic affairs of life.

It's not for us to retain *Him!*

To grasp and cling is to *lose* in divine things.

CHAPTER 11 – ESPOUSED (LEGALLY ENGAGED)

If we release ourselves to Him and learn to "let go and let Him," then *He* will abide with us, taking care of all of our needs and becoming the very fulfillment of all our desires.

Here is another great statement that took me a long time to learn:

> "His **character** and His **Word** are more important than His manifestations, His blessings or His gifts."

We must learn this—especially people (like me) from the "Spirit-filled" ranks of the Church! *He* is more important than all that is His.

> "Having been **buried with Him**…ye were also **raised with Him** through faith in the working of God, Who raised Him from the dead." (Colossians 2:12, emphasis mine)

Over time I discovered that if I can just find *Him*, then I will automatically get all that other stuff that He promised to "add unto me" in Matthew 6:33. As a bonus, He will only "add" something to me in its proper place and time.

THE POWER OF HIS RESURRECTION

> "I adjure (charge —KJV) you, O daughters…that ye stir not up, nor awaken love, until **she** [it] please." (Song of Solomon 3:5, insert mine)

When the Shulamite finally finds Him, He turns and says, "I adjure you, O daughters, that you stir not up nor awaken love until it please" (v. 3:5).

As we noted earlier, Keil & Delitzsch say the Hebrew words and context here actually say, "Until *she* please." In other words, don't stir her up until she's ready, until she's fit.

Now, this is only the second of four statements like this where the Beloved issues instructions concerning the Shulamite woman (see 2:7; 3:5; 5:8; and 8:4).

In the context of the Song of Solomon revealing the greater truth of the Lord's relationship with His Bride ......

The Risen Lord again forbids the "daughters" to touch the one in His keeping.

Something is happening in the Shulamite's life; she is really absorbing the lessons she's learned up to this point.

Sins are relative.

THE CLOSER ONE'S UNION WITH THE LORD IS, THE GREATER THE IMPACT OF SIN ON ONE'S LIFE.

Yes, sins are relative in the sense that the closer one's union with the Lord, the greater is the impact and gravity of even the least of sins.

While most people might consider a certain act to be a mere trifle, a soul in deep *union* with her Lord might consider it to be a *serious and distance-creating* act.

Such a soul cannot excuse the smallest disobedience or lack of sensitivity to His will.

Sin is any act of turning your back on Him and His ways. It doesn't have to be an outrageous crime such as rape, murder, incest or theft or robbery.

The closer you are to Him, the more conscious you are of sin.

The Lord knows this and so He provides us with times of *intimacy* and rest on a regular basis so that our spirits will not faint.

CHAPTER 11 – ESPOUSED (LEGALLY ENGAGED)

God is so good. This is why He said:

"For I will not contend forever, neither will I be always wroth: for the spirit should fail before Me, and the souls which I have made." **(Isaiah 57:16)**

In other words, God says, "I'm not going to keep on pushing you or being angry with you. Nor will I remain absent from you. I'll be there."

Listen, I want to share a crucial truth with you!

The Beloved would have come back to where the Shulamite was if she had *not* followed Him to a higher level! That may sound wonderful, but it is actually a potential tragedy in the making.

He would have accommodated Himself to her, all the way down to the passing moments of visitation (such as that illustrated by the lame man in John 5 who waited in vain for 38 years for "the troubling of the water" once a year hoping to be healed—until Christ the Healer called him higher with a life-changing question: "Wilt thou be whole?").

God will accommodate Himself to a relationship with you *at whatever level* you are willing to go. However, He wants you at the deepest and fullest level.

He will draw you as high as He can, but He will come back to the "old campfire" where you've made your permanent camp to avoid losing you altogether.

This is a great tragedy, and I'm sad to say that most Christians have made "safe" or "comfortable" choices that brought them this second-best experience. They are not willing to be everything that God has called, designed, and destined them to be. That leaves

God no choice but to accommodate Himself to their lower level of relationship.

He would take us quickly through the *12 Stairsteps* into bridehood *if we could just let go and let Him*! He doesn't want to wait, but He does because *we* are the ones who need the time to wait.

He speaks to the "daughters" that they not disturb "until she (it) please." (It is fitting, appropriate.)

Since the Shulamite woman needs more time, He speaks to the daughters and says, "Don't disturb until the time is right."

The Lord knows that He is drawing the Shulamite into the Valley of Trouble because it will be the door to fuller union with Him.

It is there that He will truly *betroth* (espouse) her to Himself.

It is in the "Valley of Trouble" that the Beloved will "betroth" her to Himself. This amounts to a "legal engagement for marriage" in which He makes her *"the one chosen."*

Hosea the prophet paints this scene *two hundred years* before Solomon's time:

> "Therefore, behold, I will allure her, and bring her into the **wilderness**, and speak comfortably unto her...
>
> "...And I will give her her vineyards from thence, and the **valley of Achor** [trouble] for a door of hope: and she shall sing there, as in the days of her youth, and as in the days when she came up out of the land of Egypt...
>
> "...And it shall be at that day, saith the LORD, that thou shalt call me **Ishi**; and shalt call me no more Baali ...
>
> "I will even betroth thee unto Me in faithfulness: and thou shalt know [yada] the LORD." (Hosea 2:14–16, 20, emphasis and parenthetic insertions mine)

CHAPTER 11 – ESPOUSED (LEGALLY ENGAGED)

If Hosea wrote this before Solomon penned the Song, then *this vision of the transformation of a divine betrothal relationship* had been a part of the metaphor and the culture of Israel *for 200 years* by the time the Beloved described how he drew the Shulamite into the wilderness.

It seems unbelievable, but it is true. It is there in the wilderness that she will learn to call Him *"Ishi"* instead of *"Baali."*

The translated meanings of those unfamiliar masculine nouns bring fresh prophetic meaning to this declaration: *"She will learn to call Him **'my husband; my man'** instead of **'my Lord'.'"***

Most of us are religious, meaning we have a certain formality and form to our faith. But the Lord is saying through Hosea the prophet that the nation of Israel, and later through the Song that the Bride of Christ "… will not just relate to Me as Lord, but she is going to relate to Me as husband, as one [with Me]."

Most of us have to admit that we tend to behave one way at church and another way in our homes. He wants us to walk with Him in the same way no matter *where* we are.

The Lord wants to make us to become so comfortable with Him that we don't even think about dividing our thinking and behavior into "sacred and profane" partitions.

It reminds me of life in the Garden of Eden before the "Fall," when Adam and Eve knew nothing about divisions between "good and evil." All they knew was union and communion with God.

Perhaps when we actually reach maturity in Christ Jesus, we won't know anything about sacred versus profane or natural and spiritual. Nor will we *care* because it simply isn't an issue.

THE MAKING OF A BRIDE

In the same way, we shouldn't care about false divisions between "laymen" and ordained ministers. We are *all* ordained. We are all called. We are all anointed. We are all ministers.

It is here in the *wilderness* with her Beloved that a dramatic transformation in the Shulamite's life takes place:

- *Out of the "wilderness"* come *her* vineyards. In other words, it is in this place of separation with Him that she perceives and receives her *ministry, calling,* and *anointing.*
- *Out of the "Valley of Trouble"* comes *a* **door** *of hope.* And as a result, *she shall sing* **there**.
- Just as the Children of Israel were free when they came out of Egypt, *she* was *free, leaving her bondage behind.* Her *"enemies"* from the past were "drowned and dead" to her. And she became *rich*, just as the Israelites brought Egypt's treasure with them.
- And finally, it was in the wilderness that she came to *know—yada—*become one with her Beloved as "Adam *knew* Eve and she bore a son...."

THE GOAL OF TRUE MATURITY IN CHRIST IS TO BECOME ONE WITH HIM.

-This is the whole thought that the Song of Solomon repeats here.

The goal of true maturity in Christ is to *know the Lord,* to experience Him by becoming *one* with Him. That is the meaning of the Hebrew word, *yada.*

When Adam *knew* Eve, what happened? She gave birth to a son. God wants to make His Betrothed one no longer a virgin, but a bride.

The Beloved will always deal *rightly* with His own.

CHAPTER 11 – ESPOUSED (LEGALLY ENGAGED)

The Lord deals rightly with His own. In other words, *we are safe in His nail-pierced hands.*

We don't need all of the answers, and we don't need to understand everything that He is doing. We just need Him, and we need to hold onto Him and what we already know of Him.

Let Him lead you. Don't make Him accommodate to your level—it may well be the last and worst thing you need in your life! Believe and trust in Him, and He will help you rise to His level and vision for your life.

> *"A bruised reed shall He not break, and the **smoking flax** shall He not quench: He shall bring forth judgment unto truth [victory]."*   (Isaiah 42:3, parenthetical insertion mine)

THE MAKING OF A BRIDE

Ch. 11 – End Notes – Espoused (Legally Engaged)

1. St. Augustine wrote his classic work, *Confessions*, about 400 years after Jesus' ascension. At the beginning of his work he says to God, *"You have made us for yourself, and our hearts are rest-less till they find their rest in you."* *Confessions* (1.1.1)

2. Blaise Pascal lived in the 1600s, and he wrote in his classic work, *Pensees*: "What else does this craving, and this helplessness, proclaim but that there was once in man a true happiness, of which all that now remains is the empty print and trace? This he tries in vain to fill with everything around him, seeking in things that are not there the help he cannot find in those that are, though none can help, since this infinite abyss can be filled only with an infinite and immutable object; in other words by God himself" (148/428).

CHAPTER 12

STAIRSTEP 9
TRANSFIGURED BY HIM

TRANSPORTED TO THE WEDDING (PROCESSIONAL)

SONG OF SOLOMON 3:6-11

"Who is this that cometh up out of the wilderness like pillars of smoke, perfumed with myrrh and frankincense?"
(Song of Solomon 3:6)

God moves quickly once we are ready!

After He engages and transfigures her in the wilderness, notice how quickly the Beloved moves the Shulamite woman into preparation for the wedding.

Gaze through the eyes of the Beloved as He talks about His bride-to-be. Now look again through the eternal lens of our God who declares "the end from the beginning"[1] and understand that He is speaking prophetically through Solomon to describe the Bride of Christ. It is marvelous and magnificent who we have become in Him!

Once again, let me say plainly that Solomon's Song doesn't tell us what happened in the wilderness. All we know is that *she was with Him in the wilderness.*

THE MAKING OF A BRIDE

Each of our individual experiences with Him is unique, personal, and unlike the experience of anyone else at any time. We will have some of the major things in common to be sure, but we are not transformed into His image merely through some kind of "cosmic cookie cutter." We are all hand-fashioned by Him for His divine purposes to be members of His Bride.

Once we are legally engaged to Him, He will deal with us as we need. This only happens when we totally submit to Him and surrender our lives in His hands. Then He will transfigure us, and quickly.

Some of the things in *your* life may be okay with Him, while those *same things* in *my* life might need His healing or corrective touch. If that is so, He will have to work on me at a level totally unnecessary for you. On the other hand, there may be problems in your life that aren't problems in mine.

Again, the Scriptures don't offer us many details about what the Beloved did with the Shulamite woman in the wilderness, but we *do* know she was transfigured when she returned.

After the "rest," she emerges from the wilderness and the "daughters" see her and glorify God in her.

Whatever happened in the wilderness, we know that the same virgins who had personally lived, walked, and talked with the Shulamite over a period of years suddenly exclaimed when they saw her:

> *"**Who is this** that cometh up out of the wilderness like pillars of smoke, perfumed with myrrh and frankincense?*
> *" (Song of Solomon 3:6, emphasis mine)*

CHAPTER 12 – TRANSPORTED TO THE WEDDING

This may sound strange, but clearly these eyewitnesses understand that the Shulamite is a new person. One reason she is different is because she has a new purpose—she is on her way to a wedding now.

They had known of her sorrow and desperation.

They saw her struggles and shortcomings over the years, but something is *different* now! When they see her *after the time spent alone with Him*, even their reaction to her changes. This is a clue to how dramatic her transfiguration was to them!

Now they say, "Who is this?" What a *change* has taken place!

"Who in the world is this? What change has taken place in you?" they ask her. Whatever the Beloved did during that time alone in the wilderness, it *transformed* and *transfigured her*. That was His purpose.

The virgins said, *"Who is this* that cometh up out of the wilderness like pillars of smoke?" Does this peculiar phrase remind you of anything?

Do you remember how God guided Moses and the Hebrews out of Egypt and through the wilderness? He did it by His Spirit in the form of "a pillar of cloud by day and fire by night."

> *"And the Lord went before them by day in a pillar of a cloud, to lead them the way; and by night in a pillar of fire, to give them light; to go by day and night:*
>
> *"He took not away the* **pillar of the cloud** *by day, nor the pillar of fire by night, from before the people."* (Exodus 13:21-22)

THE MAKING OF A BRIDE

The prophet Joel described how God would lead His people in the latter days by His Spirit, illuminating our passage in the Song in the process:

> *"And it shall come to pass afterward, that **I will pour out My Spirit upon all flesh;** and your sons and your daughters shall prophesy, your old men shall dream dreams, your young men shall see visions:*
>
> *"And also upon the servants and upon the handmaids in those days will I pour out My Spirit."* (Joel 2:28–29, emphasis mine)

This is the anointing of God revealed in the Shulamite's life (and in the Bride of Christ in the earth)!

These prophetic passages from the Old Testament show us the imagery of what happened in the wilderness with the Beloved! It is a picture of Jesus Christ so filling His Espoused with His Spirit and His life that when she emerges from the wilderness of transformation there is a divine "fragrance" and "smoke" all around her.

She emerges in the power and *anointing* of the Holy Spirit!

Applying this transformation to the life of an individual disciple of Christ, once the power and anointing of the Holy Spirit comes upon her:

- She will never be the same again!

- She will never be the "average Christian" again! Watchman Nee's book, *The Normal Christian Life,* comes to mind.

- She will forever carry this transformation with her.

- All will know she is "different."

CHAPTER 12 – TRANSPORTED TO THE WEDDING

It is worth going through the wilderness to receive this.

It's worth everything to receive this. Whatever God must to do to you to make you like this, please let Him do it. Let go and let God!

> *"Who is this that cometh out of the wilderness* **like pillars of smoke***..."*   *(Song of Solomon 3:6a, emphasis mine)*

The Shulamite woman is not only "coming out" or coming up from the wilderness. The Bible says something startling in this verse when it says she is coming out "like pillars of smoke."

Have you ever heard of the ancient Hebrew word *shekinah* or *shachan(y)ah*? It is a compound word, or a term made of two or more words.

Yah is "Yahweh," or God. "*Shachan*" refers to "the bearer or the carrier of God." It's the tabernacle or the vessel in which God travels. Rabbis used this term to describe the Presence of the Lord that hovered or "abided" over the Ark of the Covenant, positioned between the cherubim and the seraphim at the mercy seat.

We believe that Jesus literally became our living mercy seat—our propitiation (our *atonement* for our sins), our *hilasterion* (Greek) and *kippur* (Hebrew for "our atoning redemption"). All of that is involved in His indwelling or "abiding" presence through the Holy Spirit.

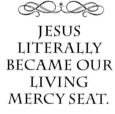

JESUS LITERALLY BECAME OUR LIVING MERCY SEAT.

I started preaching revivals when I was around 14 or 15 years old. When a little country church would invite me to preach, I'd steal away somewhere to pray and study all day before I'd preach that night. I used to pray and pound on the benches while praying in all sincerity, "Lord, send the *shekinah*."

Today, I don't pray those prayers anymore because God said to me, "You *are* the *shekinah*. *You* must **be** *the vessel in which I come."*

This "shekinah" that Solomon and the prophets described so long ago is *ours* today in Christ Jesus. It isn't just an experience. It comes through us when we yield fully to God.

This is what caused the transformation in the Shulamite woman and caused her to come back **AS the *shekinah* of God.** *Again, it is worth going through the wilderness to receive this.*

If you look closely, you see that something in or on the Shulamite woman that comes from her presence powerfully affects those around her. The Bible says she is *perfumed with myrrh.*

> *"Who is this that cometh out of the wilderness like pillars of smoke,* **perfumed** *with* **myrrh** *and* **frankincense**, *with all powders of the merchant?"*
> *(Song of Solomon 3:6-7, emphasis mine)*

She is perfumed with *myrrh*.

What is myrrh and what is its importance in the Scriptures? It was one of the ingredients of the compounded anointing oil reserved exclusively for service to God in the Tabernacle and later the Temple. Its components are detailed in Exodus 33.

Myrrh was also:

- One of the three extravagant gifts (along with gold and frankincense) given by the Magi to the infant Jesus in Bethlehem (Matthew 2:11).

- Offered to Jesus during the crucifixion process, but He refused to accept it, possibly because it was mixed with wine (something He said He wouldn't drink until the Kingdom had

CHAPTER 12 – TRANSPORTED TO THE WEDDING

fully come), and because myrrh might have helped relieve or deaden the pain (Mark 15:22-24).

- Brought by Joseph of Arimathaea and Nicodemus for the burial of Jesus' body after His death on the Cross (John 19:38-40).

The predominant imagery of myrrh in the Scriptures seems to involve death, and what it means to become alive to God.

What happened in the wilderness with the Beloved? The Shulamite died to herself and came alive to Him and in Him.

The fragrance of myrrh is released only after the bark of the *Commiphora Myrrha* tree is cut, causing the plant to "bleed" or exude its bitter sap or resin. In the same way, the "tender plant" or "root" of the Lord was wounded, bruised, and "cut" for our transgressions. It is "by His stripes" that we are healed!

> *"For He shall grow up before Him **as a tender plant**, and as **a root out of a dry ground:** He hath no form nor comeliness; and when we shall see Him, there is no beauty that we should desire Him...*
>
> *"Yet it pleased the LORD to **bruise** Him; He hath put Him to grief: when thou shalt make His soul an offering for sin, He shall see His seed, He shall prolong His days, and the pleasure of the LORD shall prosper in His hand."*
>
> (Isaiah 53:2, 10; emphasis mine)

There is a special "fragrance from cutting" that is released only when we die to self and become "alive in Him."

Even in Jacob's life, we see how a "loser and trickster from birth" became "a leader with a limp" through his dealings with God in a wilderness place in times of struggle.

THE MAKING OF A BRIDE

She smells also of *frankincense*.

Frankincense is an aromatic resin produced from the sap obtained from trees of the genus Boswellia in the family Burseraceae.

The resin was pounded or beaten until it was pulverized, and then infused with oil or water to produce one of the most priceless of fragrances. One of the most unique qualities of frankincense is that the aroma contained in its liquid-distilled gum is *released when it is crushed.*

Frankincense, along with myrrh, was a key ingredient for the holy anointing oil and incense used in sacred worship in the Tabernacles of Moses and David and Solomon's Temple. It represents brokenness, pliability, and the process of melting in the presence of fire.

A DESIRABLE FRAGRANCE RISES FROM THE FIRES OF BROKENNESS.

In the Song, the Bride is pictured as melted, broken and pliable in the presence of her Beloved. A sweet and desirable fragrance rises from the fire of her trials and brokenness.

Brokenness is the key to advancement in God throughout the Scriptures, and this is what she was. *Whatever He did to the Shulamite in the wilderness transformed and transfigured her and got her ready for a wedding.*

Isn't that what God is doing with us today? I am convinced it is.

THE VICTORIOUS SOUL

"Behold, it is the litter [bed] of Solomon; threescore mighty men are about it.... All handle the sword and are expert in war. Every man hath his sword...because of fear in the night."

(Song of Solomon 3:7–8)

CHAPTER 12 – TRANSPORTED TO THE WEDDING

Through her wilderness experience with the Beloved, she is transfigured and now He is bringing her back home.

The "daughters" say, "Who is this?" Then they add, "It is the *bed* of Solomon!"

We hear the daughters say, "Who is this?" in verse 6 and the amazing answer is, "It's the bed of Solomon."

When the bed of Solomon comes into sight, we are told it is surrounded by 60 mighty men who are all armed experts of war "because of fear in the night."

Wait a minute: how is the Shulamite bride being transported from the wilderness? The answer is literally "on the bed of Solomon."

It is a triumphant procession emerging from the wilderness—Solomon's bed guarded by *warriors*.

What exquisite imagery! Some say this refers to Jesus emerging from the wilderness after His conflict with Satan, but I don't agree. We find a far better picture of a triumphant King marching toward His wedding celebration in Paul's letter to the church at Colossae:

> *"[Jesus blotted] out the handwriting of ordinances that was against us...and took it out of the way, nailing it to His cross;*
>
> *"And having spoiled principalities and powers, He made a show of them openly, triumphing over them in it."*
> (Colossians 2:14–15)

As she abides in intimate union with her Lord, she will be carried safely over "the wiles of the devil."

As we've seen from the earlier chapters in the Song of Solomon, the "bed" is symbolic of total *submission* to Him. It symbolizes being in the harem (Heb. - *charem* - set apart from all others unto the beloved, although the wedding had not yet officially taken place, nor been consummated in intercourse.)

As you live in communion with the Lord as part of His *Bride*, you are at the same time a *mighty warrior*. As the Church, we together are His Bride, His lover, and at the same time His representative in the earth.

At that level of healthy relationship you can't have an affair. This is a picture of a husband and wife in union, where the two have become one.

As the Bride abides in intimate union with her Lord, she will be carried safely over the wiles of the devil. This picture of the bridal bed portrays total submission to the Beloved.

To be transparently honest, when you climb into bed with somebody—and it really should be your *spouse*—you are absolutely defenseless against him. If he or she wants to hurt you, then he or she can hurt you.

The truth is that this new bride has no power in and of herself. Frankly, she is defenseless *unless* He is lying in the bed with her!

The good news is that *as we are in communion with Him, God will encamp around us with guardian* **angels**. As we live in union with Him, He supplies our provision and protection. We see a glimpse of the awesome power God unleashes in a fight in the Book of Revelation:

> "There was war in heaven: Michael and his angels fought against the dragon; and the dragon fought, and his angels."
> (Revelation 12:7)

Believe me, spiritual warfare is real. Paul assured us from hard experience:

CHAPTER 12 – TRANSPORTED TO THE WEDDING

> *"For we wrestle not against flesh and blood, but against principalities, against powers, against the rulers of the darkness of this world, against spiritual wickedness in high places."*
> (Ephesians 6:12)

This warfare is real, but we don't need to worry because we are in union with Him! We have 60 angelic warriors, "clever in the sword," or whatever cosmic weaponry they use, protecting us.

THE GOD-POSSESSED SOUL

> *"King Solomon made himself a [carriage of state] of the **wood** of Lebanon…the pillars thereof of silver, the bottom…of **gold**, the seat of it of **purple**, the midst thereof being **inlaid with love**, from the daughters of Jerusalem."*
> (Song of Solomon 3:9–10, emphasis mine)

Did you notice how Solomon's bridal bed is transformed into a chariot right in front of our eyes? It seems that King Solomon himself made a "royal chariot" or "official state car" from the legendary wood of Lebanon. The Scriptures describe the transformation in incredible detail as if on purpose.

If you still don't believe that this is a metaphor and allegory, and that virtually everything in the Song of Solomon is symbolic, then picture this chariot.

In quick review, this official state carriage is made out of cedar wood. The pillars are silver, the bottom is gold, the seat is purple, and "the midst of it," the middle of this royal chariot—where your feet would stay—is *love*.

It is symbolic. We have to remember that as we go forward.

The daughters of Jerusalem now see the *glory* of God upon her as she is *united with Him in His resurrection*.

THE MAKING OF A BRIDE

This woman is not the same person they once knew. Now it is clear to all who look at her that she has taken on the glory and wonder of her husband, the King. She is miraculously transformed as she is united with Him in this resurrection.

This is a public show and victory procession. She has become one with Him now. She is His. She is on her way to being the bride. She's not yet the bride, but she's on her way now.

They see that she is entirely His *workmanship*.

As the Apostle Paul told the Ephesian church, "*We* [the individual members of His Church and Bride] *are His workmanship, created in Christ Jesus for good works ...*" (Ephesians 2:10, emphasis and insertion mine).

The Beloved in the Song took His bride-to-be into that wilderness and transfigured her for something special. The next thing we know the virgins are speaking of His bridal bed as a chariot!

Now they speak of His chariot.

It is easy to see that He is describing *more* than some ephemeral bed chariot; He is describing *her*.

She is His *bed/chariot*. They are now seeing the Shulamite woman as both His *bride/warrior* in battle and His *wife/partner* in ministry.

The chariot—the Beloved's vehicle in which He has His habitation and transport is described in detail. It is a description of the *soul* of His *love*.

Why is the chariot described in such detail? It is because it is a description of *the soul of His love*. Our eternal souls and spirits live *with Christ* in our temporary earthly bodies.

CHAPTER 12 – TRANSPORTED TO THE WEDDING

Jesus, our risen Lord and the Bridegroom of the Church, no longer walks the earth. He lives *in us* by His Spirit as we walk out His purposes in this life together.

This Resurrected Jesus shares an intimate marriage relationship with only *one Bride* in the earth.

Who is called and empowered to be His representative in the earth, to conquer the kingdoms of this world and make them the kingdoms of our God and of His Christ?

That privilege and responsibility belongs solely to The Bride of Christ, His Church. As Paul explained to the Corinthian believers:

> *"For we know that if our earthly house of this tabernacle [our physical bodies] were dissolved, we have a building of God, a house not made with hands, eternal in the heavens."*
>
> (2 Corinthians 5:1)

For this reason, the detailed description of the Beloved's chariot reveals a wealth of wisdom for us right now, in *this* life we share with Christ Jesus.

The "wood of Lebanon" speaks of her *humanity*—of the earth, earthy.

Wood is earthy. You don't see wood in biblical descriptions of heaven, except perhaps in descriptions of the Tree of Life in The Revelation. Generally, wood is considered to concern things that are earthy, or "of the earth."

The Bride of Christ is composed of the *earthy redeemed* souls of humankind, of people who were born, breathed air, and lived on the earth. Even the angels of heaven are not included in this unique Church of the Redeemed.

The "pillars of silver" speak of her *redemption* by the precious blood of Jesus.

Silver speaks of *ransom* and *redemption*. Specifically it represents blood redemption in the Scriptures. Under the Old Testament law, every firstborn was redeemed with five shekels of silver (see Numbers 18:15-16).

The "gold" speaks of the *divine* life of the indwelling Lord.

Gold speaks of divinity.

The "purple seat" speaks of His royal throne as *King*.

The color purple speaks of royalty, and has done so from antiquity. In some cultures and eras, this color was reserved solely for royalty. The purple seat speaks of a king's regal throne and royalty.

The Temple is spoken of as the place of His feet which is the "midst paved with *love* of the daughters of Jerusalem."

The cabin/temple of the Beloved's carriage or bed/chariot dwelling is filled with love. This speaks of the love of the Church.

THE CROWNED CHRIST

> *"Go forth, O ye **daughters of Zion**, and behold **KING SOLOMON** …crowned … **in the day of His espousals**, and in the day of the gladness of His heart."*
> (Song of Solomon 3:11, emphasis mine)

Finally, we see that King Solomon is now crowned and the Shulamite woman is his transfigured Bride. He is crowned because this is the day of his "espousal," where he takes his betrothed love as his espoused bride.

CHAPTER 12 – TRANSPORTED TO THE WEDDING

Why is this "day of his espousal" also called "the day of the gladness of his heart"? It is because at last, on this special day, he finally receives His mature and ready bride!

King Solomon in the Song was and is a picture and prophetic portrait of the Risen Lord who will one day receive His mature and ready Bride and celebrate the Marriage Supper of the Lamb.

The daughters of *Zion* — who are they?

> *"Ye are come unto [Mount Zion], and unto the city of the living God, the heavenly Jerusalem, and to an innumerable company of angels."*
> (Hebrews 12:22–23, parenthetical insertion mine).

Who are these "daughters of Zion" in Song of Solomon 3:11? They are the virgins representing all the people of the church. They are *not* the Bride, but the Bride of the Lamb does come from this larger group just as the Shulamite woman rose from among the virgins to become Solomon's royal bride.

> *"But ye are come unto [Mount Zion], and unto the city of the living God, the heavenly Jerusalem, and to an innumerable company of angels,*
>
> **"To the general assembly and church of the firstborn**, *which are written in heaven, and to God the Judge of all, and to the spirits of just men made perfect."*
> (Hebrews 12:22-23, bold emphasis and parenthetical insertion mine)

"Zion" is not the Church, but the *destination* of the Church and every believer in it. It represents our place of destiny or fulfilled purpose.

Our supreme example and pioneer of faith, Jesus Christ, *reached His "earthly Zion"* on The Cross when He shouted, *"It is finished!"*

THE MAKING OF A BRIDE

*"Go forth, O ye daughters of Zion, and b***ehold King Solomon...** *crowned...in the day of His espousals,* *and in the day of the gladness of His heart."* (Song of Solomon 3:11, emphasis mine)

These are told to look upon her, for she has become a *crown* upon His royal brow.

Understand that God, through Solomon, is talking about *the Bride's transformation* while drawing from many biblical references. He is specifically describing her "Zion," or her divine destiny in Him.

You won't understand the deeper meaning of the command to the virgins to "behold king Solomon *with the crown* wherewith his mother crowned him *in the day of his espousals*" unless you draw on a Messianic revelation of Isaiah the prophet made nearly 200 years later.

In Isaiah 62, the prophet pictures a redeemed Israel, a spiritual Bride composed of Jews and Gentiles transformed by the Messiah:

*"****Thou*** *shalt also be **a crown of glory** in the hand of the Lord and a royal diadem in the hand of thy God. You will be no more termed* ***Forsaken***.*"* (Isaiah 62:3-4a, italic emphasis mine)

The writer in the Song is actually telling the virgins, "Look upon her (the Shulamite bride). Look upon her for *she* has become *a crown upon His royal brow."* Wow.

"But Dr. Cottle, *you're not being logical here. I'm having a hard time following all of this."* Of course. Remember that the Song is greatly symbolic by divine design! Don't expect it to fit neatly into logical categories according to our Western mindset.

- First, we see her as the *shekinah* (the "tabernacle or the vessel in which God travels").

CHAPTER 12 – TRANSPORTED TO THE WEDDING

- Then she is the fragrance of *myrrh* and *frankincense*.

- Almost immediately, she becomes the Beloved's *bed*, and then His *warrior chariot*.

- Now she becomes the *crown* on His brow.

All of these scriptural revelations and references are incorporated into this incredible composite picture. Frankly, you must be steeped in the Scriptures to have any understanding of the Song of Solomon.

It is worth persevering and "studying the Scriptures" to show yourself approved as you rightly divide and understand God's will for the Church in the earth.[2]

There is a promise attached to perseverance that applies to all who love the King of kings and are committed to seeing the Kingdom of His Father come and His will be done on the earth as it is in heaven:

> *"Him that overcometh will I make a pillar in the temple of my God."*   (Revelation 3:12)

A pillar in the Temple of God is a weight-bearing support representing and operating supernaturally as His strength pursuing and accomplishing God's purpose in the earth.

The soul now moves into a new dimension of *favor* with her Beloved.

THE MAKING OF A BRIDE

End Notes – Ch. 12 – Transported to the Wedding

1. See Isaiah 46:10.
2. See 2 Timothy 2:15.

STAGE D

WEDDING

FROM WEDDING PREPARATION TO BRIDE AND PARTNER

The Tenth Stairstep – Exalted by Him

Chapter 13 – Prepared & Exalted for the Wedding (Ready)

Chapter 14 – The New Creation in Christ

The Eleventh Stairstep - Seated in the Heavens with Him

Chapter 15 – Enthroned (Established)

The Twelfth Stairstep – Serving Others with Him

Chapter 16 – Bride (Partner)

THE MAKING OF A BRIDE

CHAPTER 13

STAIRSTEP 10
EXALTED BY HIM(READY)

PREPARED AND EXALTED FOR THE WEDDING

SONG OF SOLOMON 4:1-5

"Behold, thou art fair, my love." (Song of Solomon 4:1)

The Soul now moves into a new dimension of favor in the Beloved. To borrow a phrase from Paul's letter to the Ephesians, God is "raising her up and making her to sit in heavenly places in Christ Jesus" (see Ephesians 2:6).

The soul is now seated with the Beloved in the heavenly places.

We're at the first verse of Chapter 4, just one short chapter away from the conclusion of the first half of this wonderful book. At last, the soul is now seated with the Beloved in the heavenlies.

The Beloved now opens His heart to His loved one as He could never do before.

She is legally engaged to Him, she has been transfigured and made ready for Him. Now He will say things to her and about her that really prepare her for the wedding that will make her His bride.

In the time of quiet which followed the conflict in the wilderness, she learned her greatest lesson, and that is to be silent before Him.

Earlier she "talked too much" and He spoke only briefly.

Before her time in the wilderness, the Shulamite woman talked long and often about her experiences, impressions, fears, and feelings. "Oh, I got blessed, I got this, I did that."

This is acceptable at a certain stage, but maturity brings greater responsibility and wisdom.

Now she enters His presence and listens for Him to speak.

This is a sign of *maturity* and *humility*. It reveals a totally different dimension in her relationship with the Beloved.

David captured and expressed this dimension in Psalms 62:5: "My soul wait thou only upon God, for my expectation is from Him."

This is the *silence* and reverence of godly awe. Sadly, this is "learned behavior" for most of us humans, especially those of us who are Americans.

As for the Bible, it declares, *"The Lord is in His holy temple; let all the earth **keep silence** before Him"* (Habakkuk 2:20).

He speaks from the deep hush of the sanctuary within her soul.

CHAPTER 13 – THE HEAVENLY LIFE

Now He starts telling her wonderful things about herself. Ironically, the Beloved's first words to her mark the place where many "modern" people lose their interest in Song of Solomon because they see this statement as "sexist."

This view is ridiculous and reveals a serious misunderstanding of ancient Semitic culture and sacred writings. He said…

"Thou art fair."

As we learned earlier, when the Beloved tells the Shulamite wife-to-be she is *fair,* he is also saying much more than "You are beautiful." He is also saying she is transparent and vulnerable to him in their intimate relationship unlike any other.

On an entirely different level, when the Lord speaks to us, His word is *creative.* It *makes us* what He calls us (see Romans 4:17)!

Normally she would have replied to the Beloved's compliment by saying, said, "Oh, wonderful." Notice that she didn't say a word. She finally landed on the right response—silence.

Do you remember Mary's humble response to the Archangel Gabriel's astounding and frightening message to her from God? She simply said, "Be it unto me according to Thy Word" (Luke 2:38).

As a result, the Holy Spirit hovered over her and supernaturally impregnated her with Emmanuel—*God with Us.* It is precisely this kind of humble, submissive prayer and heart attitude that "births Christ-in-us"!

She no longer turns to *herself* for evidence. Instead, she judges Him faithful and His Word sufficient.

He is faithful and what He says about me is true, regardless of what anybody else says, or even what I think about it.

She is the "Sea of Crystal" before His throne and at His feet (Revelation 4:6). Remember that we are dealing with a God who... "Calleth those things that are not, as though they were" (Romans 4:17b). He is the One Who said, "Let there be," and it was so (see Genesis 1:6-7).

In other words, *all things leaped from His Word!*

This is the "hearing of faith" that obtains the *promise*.

The Apostle Peter put it this way in his second letter to the churches:

> *"Through the knowledge of Him that has called us to glory and virtue: Whereby are given unto us exceeding great and precious promises that by these ye might be partakers of the divine nature."* (2 Peter 1:3-4)

You see, whatever He says about her she hears, incorporates, and incarnates (or *embodies*) in her life and becomes a partaker of the divine nature. This is *her "Amen" to His "Yea"* (see 2 Corinthians 1:20)!

> *"For how many soever be the promises of God, in Him is the **yea**: wherefore also through Him [working in us] is the Amen, unto the glory of God through us."*
> (2 Corinthians 1:20, ASV, italic emphasis and parenthetical insertion mine)

The Bible says in Psalm 65:1, "There shall be *silence* before Thee, and *praise*, O God, in *Zion*" (emphasis mine). Remember that "Zion" pictures the *destiny* of the individual believer and the Church.

It seems that by and large, many of us "modern" believers don't understand silent praise. We think praise is noisy, but this isn't always true.

CHAPTER 13 – THE HEAVENLY LIFE

Praise is, in its simplest form, any type of adoration, adulation, and thanksgiving for everything He is speaking into our lives. It springs up naturally as we become what He says.

"Thou art fair, My *love*."

These are the words of the *Risen Lord* to His redeemed one as he describes the characteristics of the new life in union with Him.

How does He transfigure her?

We know she is not fair in herself but only in *Him*. So how does He exalt her and change her into His bride? He does it by speaking.

Why are we surprised? The Scriptures plainly tell us He has created everything by the word of His power and He upholds everything by the word of His power (see Colossians 1:15-17, Hebrews 1:3). Of course He does it by *speaking*.

This is when He begins to describe His new creation in the Shulamite–her new identity "in Christ" so to speak. As Paul said in his second letter to the Corinthians:

> *"If any man be in Christ, he is a new creature, old things are passed away; behold, all things are become new."*
> (2 Corinthians 5:17)

The new life must "grow up into Him in all things [to the measure of His growth]" (Ephesians 4:15).

After all, He is the "champion who initiates and perfects our faith" (Hebrews 12:2, NLT), and according to Paul, Jesus Christ represents "the fullness of the Godhead bodily" (Colossians 2:9). How could there be any other measure or source for our growth?

THE MAKING OF A BRIDE

God gives the blueprint and the "Yea;" her part is "to add all diligence" and say "Amen," so that at His appearing she may be found "perfect and entire, lacking *nothing*" (James 1:4).

The New International Version of the Bible puts it this way: "Perseverance must finish its work so that you may be *mature* and *complete*, not lacking anything."

Chapter 14

STAIRSTEP 10 – CONTINUED

THE NEW CREATION IN CHRIST

Notice closely how the Beloved describes the Shulamite and understand that this is a metaphorical picture of *us* as His developing Bride! This is how He sees us and what He thinks of us in Christ.

Her eyes are as *doves*.

> *"Thine eyes are as **doves** ['within thy locks' - KJV] behind thy veil."* (Song of Solomon 4:1, ASV, italic emphasis and insertion mine)

The Holy Spirit is the dove—note Jesus' baptism.

The dove is one of the most prevalent representations of the Holy Spirit in the Bible. Do you remember how the Third Person of the Trinity appears at Jesus' baptism?

> *"And Jesus, when He was baptized, went up straightway out of the water: and, lo, the heavens were opened unto him, and He saw **the Spirit of God descending like a dove**, and lighting upon Him."* (Matthew 3:16, emphasis mine)

If you recall the characteristic of paired lovebirds I mentioned earlier, they focus on each other so exclusively that it is as if they have no peripheral vision. They have eyes only for each other.

THE MAKING OF A BRIDE

When the Beloved looks at her, He sees His own spirit in her.[1]

She is a dove because she has lost the resentful spirit of the *old* life.

In her helplessness, she makes her nest only in the cleft of the *rock*. She is not out flying around sampling other possibilities.

> *"Abandon your towns and dwell among the rocks, you who live in Moab. Be **like** a dove that makes its nest **at the mouth of a cave.**"* (Jeremiah 48:28, NIV, italic emphasis mine)

Jeremiah and many of the older prophets in the Torah, along with the writings of Moses, favor the ancient Hebrew historical metaphors. Many of them show up here in the imagery of *The Song of Solomon*.

In essence, they are celebrating their cultural history and faith.

Her hair is compared to *goats* on Mount Gilead.

> *"Thy hair is as a flock of goats that appear on Mount Gilead."* (Song of Solomon 4:1, ERV – marginal notes)

This odd verse is a fitting answer to those few sadly mistaken individuals who like to claim that the Bible is "sexist literature." Think about it: once a man in our day tells a woman that her hair "is like the hair of a flock of goats," he might as well hang it up. The thrill is gone. He won't even get in the door.

Yet, that is what the "wisest man in the world" is saying to what may have been one of the most beautiful women in the ancient world: "Thy hair is as a flock of goats, that appear on mount Gilead."

What in the world does this mean? Honestly, the goats I've been around in North America tend to be smelly and somewhat

CHAPTER 14 – THE NEW CREATION IN CHRIST

obnoxious creatures. (If you have a pet goat or two, please pardon my general ignorance of their better features.)

In any case, Solomon was not talking about the goat of the western world.

The goat of the east was a stalwart creature. He was the lead animal in the flock and his hair was like fine silk. One of the letters mentioned in the Book of *Revelation* was directed to the church of Laodicea. That city was known for its unique breed of black goats that produced some of the most beautiful goat's hair in the world. They sold it around the world and it made them very, very rich.

The goat in the ancient east was a noble, clean creature, not at all like the one we know today.

Even the subject of "hair" has its own "glory" in the Scriptures, and many examples would have been embedded in the minds of Jewish people in the ancient era. For instance, as a part of the ancient Nazarite vow, anyone who took that vow would not cut his hair as a public sign marking him as separated unto God.

Judges 16 introduces us to Samson, chosen by God and endowed with supernatural strength to be a judge over Israel. He finally confessed to Delilah, his wife, after she pressed him to reveal his secret:

> "... he told her all his heart, and said unto her, There hath not come a razor upon mine head; for **I have been a Nazarite unto God** from my mother's womb: if I be shaven, then my **strength** will go from me, and I shall become weak, and be like any other man." (Judges 16:17, emphasis mine)

God's gift of supernatural strength was bound-up with Samson's hair and his Nazarite vow. It is what separated him unto God.

Absalom, the proud third son of David is another example that may well have been in Solomon's thoughts. All of Israel seemed to take pride in Prince Absalom's long, black flowing hair. It set him apart from the other sons of David.

It was as if people would tell one another, "Here is our prince, the son of David. He is going to be our next king. Just look at him: isn't it obvious that God has blessed him?"

Absalom was very proud of his hair himself, and he took every opportunity to let that hair flow for others to admire.

In his mischief and rebellion against his father, Absalom's hair became tangled in a tree while he was fleeing from King David's soldiers and that was the end of things for Absalom (see Second Samuel 18). This was part of the beautiful symbolism in the Scriptures as well.

Her strength is in the *Lord* and in the power of His might.

It is very likely that Solomon had these examples from Israel's spiritual history in mind and used them as metaphors of the Shulamite's strength in the Lord and in the power of His might.

Her teeth are compared to a flock of newly shorn *ewes*.

"Thy teeth are like a flock of ewes ... newly shorn ... *come up from the washing*, whereof every one hath twins" (Song of Solomon 4:2, emphasis mine).

Now Solomon compares the Shulamite's "teeth" to a flock of newly shorn ewes. That really will get people excited, won't it? If the ewes (female sheep) are newly shorn, it means they don't have any wool on them. It has all been cut or sheared off.

Teeth signify the *mind*—that by which we masticate and internalize food (truth).

CHAPTER 14 – THE NEW CREATION IN CHRIST

He says her teeth are like freshly shorn ewes *"coming up from the washing."* At least they're clean, and it seems that everyone has "twins." So from a strictly literal perspective, she has a whole lot of teeth that are clean.

However, we are dealing with sophisticated ancient Middle Eastern metaphor. In this portrait, teeth signify the mind. We use our minds to chew or "masticate" and internalize truth revealed in God's Word, the Gospel, the Torah, and the faith.

The mind must be clean—washed by the water of the *Word*.

Our spiritual "teeth" must be clean and "washed by the water of the word." Paul told the Ephesians, "Christ also loved the church, and gave himself for it; that he might sanctify and cleanse it *with the washing of water by the word*" (Ephesians 5:25b-26).

John declared in his first letter to the churches, "If we confess our sins, he is faithful and just to forgive us our sins, and to *cleanse us* from all unrighteousness" (1 John 1:9, emphasis mine).

The mind must be "newly *shorn*."

This is a picture of cutting away things that hinder, like a spiritual circumcision.

Priests under the Old Testament guidelines couldn't wear wool into the Holy Place within the veil. They were commanded to wear only pure linen made from flax fibers. Ezekiel the prophet tells us why:

> *"And it shall come to pass, that when they enter in at the gates of the inner court,* **they shall be clothed with linen garments; and no wool shall come upon them,** *whiles they minister in the gates of the inner court, and within.*

THE MAKING OF A BRIDE

> *"They shall have linen bonnets upon their heads, and shall have linen breeches upon their loins;* **they shall not gird themselves with any thing that causeth sweat."**
> *(Ezekiel 44:17-18, emphasis mine)*

Sweat represents human labor, human effort, and human thought. The mind, too, must be "shorn of the wisdom" of this world gained through the sweaty labor of purely human effort.

THE KINGDOM OF GOD HAS NO SELF-HELP PROGRAMS.

Only our Righteous God can make us righteous. The Kingdom has absolutely no "self-help" program to offer us. Paul said, "For *it is God* which worketh in you both *to will* and *to do* of His good pleasure" (Philippians 2:13, emphasis mine).

Christ did not come to change the culture and make us better; He came to save the race and make us new.

Human knowledge isn't inherently evil, but it has limitations! It will *always* fail to gain the knowledge of God and will come to nothing in the pursuit of truth.

Paul talks about *renewing the mind* in First Corinthians, doesn't he?

> *"And have put on the new man, which is* **renewed in knowledge** *after the image of Him that created him."*
> *(Colossians 3:10, emphasis mine)*

The Beloved is defining His bride now. By His own definition, He is preparing and transfiguring her to become all that He said. With His words, He is exalting and even "enthroning" her.

A part of that process involves renewing her mind. We must go through the same process in our own journeys with the King.

CHAPTER 14 – THE NEW CREATION IN CHRIST

The mind must be shorn of the wisdom of this world. W. J. Conybeare and J. S. Howson said in their classic 19th century work, *The Life and Epistles of St. Paul*, that the wisdom of the world "fails to gain the knowledge of God." They cite First Corinthians 1:21, which says "…it pleased God by the foolishness of preaching to save them that believe."

Conybeare and Howson also said the world's wisdom ultimately "comes to naught," citing First Corinthians 2:16: "For who hath known the mind of the Lord, that he may instruct him? But we have the mind of Christ."

Paul speaks of "renewing the mind" and a mind "renewed in knowledge."

Paul revealed in the First century that the key to our transformation into Christ's image was "the renewing of the mind."

> *"I beseech you, brethren, by the mercies of God, that ye present your bodies a living sacrifice, holy, acceptable unto God, which is your reasonable service. And be not conformed to this world: but be ye transformed by the renewing of your mind, that ye may prove what is that good, and acceptable, and perfect, will of God."* (Romans 12:1-2)

Her lips are like scarlet, the speech *comely*.

> *"Thy lips are like … scarlet … thy speech is comely."*
> (Song of Solomon 4:3 ERV, marginal notes)

If you tell a woman she has a "scarlet mouth", then don't be surprised to learn that she considers it to be an insult. In our day, this would mean, "Woman, you have too much makeup on."

That is not the case here. He said, *"Thy lips are like scarlet; thy speech is comely."*

Her lips are washed in the precious scarlet blood of Jesus so that now they speak life and not death.

Examine the passages below that I've drawn from the Book of *Isaiah* and the Book of Proverbs, and you will realize that the Beloved says the Shulamite's speech is comely, he meant much more than merely "beautiful."

Comely also means fitting, appropriate, correct, truthful, honest, and with integrity.

> *"I create the fruit of the lips; Peace, peace to him that is far off, and to him that is near, saith the LORD; and I will heal him."*
> *(Isaiah 57:19)*

> *"Life and death are in the power of the tongue."* *(Proverbs 18:21)*

Her speech is *comely*.

In other words, it is a *good* thing, and a *smart* thing to have speech that is *comely* in your life! Conybeare and Howson specifically cited Paul's counsel to the Ephesian church and to his spiritual son, Titus:

> *"Be filled with the indwelling of the Spirit when you **speak** one to another."* *(Ephesians 5:18, emphasis mine)*

> *"In all things shewing thyself **a pattern of good works:** in doctrine shewing uncorruptness, gravity, sincerity,*

> ***"Sound speech,** that cannot be condemned; that he that is of the contrary part may be ashamed, having no evil thing to say of you."* *(Titus 2:7-8, emphasis mine)*

Her temples are like a piece of a *pomegranate*.

> *"Thy temples are like a piece of a pomegranate behind thy veil."*
> *(Song of Solomon 4:3)*

CHAPTER 14 – THE NEW CREATION IN CHRIST

This is my favorite. The Beloved says her "... temples are like a piece of pomegranate."

Have you ever broken apart a pomegranate and eaten those sweet, delicate, red-colored tinted crystals inside? I know you have, and I'm salivating as I write about it. You can't help it. It's a very special fruit.

The seeds of a pomegranate are like exquisite crystal tinged in red.

This descriptive picture typifies her thought life. It is blood-washed. Delicate. Beautiful. Transparent.

What could be a more exquisite picture of pure thoughts than a pomegranate seed? This typifies the mind adorned in a meek and quiet spirit of *modesty* and inner beauty.

This also pictures the soul mind "behind the veil," signifying its hiddenness with Christ in God. Humility and modesty characterize her thought processes at this stage of her preparation.

At this stage in our own development, we would be saying, "Everything I have has been given to me by God. I didn't create any of it; therefore, I can't be praised for any of it. That is reserved solely for Him."

The beautiful and precious thoughts are veiled in quietness and modesty in her now—unlike earlier when she "talked too much" and interpreted everything in terms of *herself.*

> MATURE CHRISTIANS HAVE A SETTLED QUIETNESS AND VIRTUE OF THOUGHT.

There is a settled quietness and virtue in the thought life of mature followers of Christ. They've moved on from the shallow waters of "me" to the deeper waters of "Him."

THE MAKING OF A BRIDE

Her neck is like a *tower*.

> *"Thy neck is like the tower of David builded for an armory, whereon there hang a thousand bucklers."* (Song of Solomon 4:4)

Now we come to the "really sexist" description of the Shulamite: "[Her] *neck is like the tower of David....*"

To understand this passage you need to know what an ancient near-eastern "buckler" was and how it related to "the tower of David."

The buckler of the Roman and Medieval period was a small shield, generally made of leather or metal, that was used to parry or deflect swords, knives, and other weapons in close-quarters combat.

But the buckler of David's day was a leather harness that a warrior put over his shoulders or hung around his waist at the sash.

He attached his sword to the buckler, and might insert a scabbard for a dagger for use in hand-to-hand combat. In some cases, he would also put his bow and his quiver for his arrows on the back of that buckler.

In other words, a warrior's buckler held all the implements of his warfar*e*.

When the King's soldiers entered the palace or came into the city at night, they would *hang their bucklers on the tower of Jerusalem*. They did this because they were not allowed to have all of those weapons inside the city. The weapons on their bucklers were reserved for fighting outside the city.

> *"Thy neck is like the tower of David ... whereon there hang a thousand bucklers."*   (Song of Solomon 4:4)

CHAPTER 14 – THE NEW CREATION IN CHRIST

This does not signify that she is haughty or *obstinate* but strong.

The Beloved isn't referring to her as one who is "stiff-necked." To the contrary, he is talking about her strength.

The Beloved compares her neck to the tower of David which contained the shields of his "mighty men."

This compares to the full arsenal of His mighty men. This is a picture of the "whole armor of God."

*Her steadfast uprightness and godly character made her "mighty in battle," an invincible **warrior** in the Spirit realm.*

You see, if a soldier is willing to take off his buckler and hang it on your tower, then he trusts you not to kill him because he is totally defenseless.

If he kept his buckler in his possession, then he could harm, conquer, or kill you. But he is willing to make himself totally vulnerable.

She is prepared for battle against the hosts of darkness or whatever may encroach upon the city of peace.

Paul the apostle told us how to prepare for battle in the Book of Ephesians:

"Finally, my brethren, be strong in the Lord, and in the power of His might.

"Put on the whole armour of God, that ye may be able to stand against the wiles of the devil.

"For we wrestle not against flesh and blood, but against principalities, against powers, against the rulers of the darkness of this world, against spiritual wickedness in high places.

THE MAKING OF A BRIDE

"Wherefore take unto you the whole armour of God, that ye may be able to withstand in the evil day, and having done all, to stand.

"Stand therefore, having your loins girt about with truth, and having on the breastplate of righteousness;

"And your feet shod with the preparation of the gospel of peace;

"Above all, taking the shield of faith, wherewith ye shall be able to quench all the fiery darts of the wicked.

"And take the helmet of salvation, and the sword of the Spirit, which is the word of God." (Ephesians 6:10–17)

Her breasts are like *fawns*, feeding among lilies.

"Thy two breasts are like two fawns ... which feed among the lilies." (Song of Solomon 4:5)

Fawns are young deer.

Fawns are very young deer aged several days to one year. They are so immature that they can't reproduce yet.

The Shulamite is just now getting started. Indeed, she hasn't even reached bride status yet. The Beloved has not calling her bride yet, even though she's qualified.

I love the next point, because for years I'd watch my students write in their books with their heads down, desperately avoiding eye contact.

The "breasts" are compared to young deer that are beginning to feed on their own among tender plants. They are building up their capacity to store up revelation for sharing it with others.

The young fawns feed among the lilies (of the valley) to grow and mature so as to be able to feed babes in Christ the "sincere milk of the Word."

CHAPTER 14 – THE NEW CREATION IN CHRIST

*The fawn's breasts are small, and their capacity is **limited** now because of their lack of maturation and growth.* This is precisely the place into which the soul had now arrived. However, spring is on the way. She is getting ready to be a mother.

Daily she "... studies to show herself approved ... a workman that needs not to be ashamed, rightly dividing the Word of Truth" (see 2 Timothy 2:15).

Before this stage, she was a virgin *and* unable to reproduce. But now she is getting ready to become a bride and a mother.

Sadly, many young or long-delayed Christians find themselves stalled in the milk-fed baby place. There is nothing wrong with this as long as they don't linger there.

> "Everyone that partaketh of milk is without experience of the word of righteousness, for he is a babe."   (Hebrews 5:13, ASV)

The soul, pictured in the Shulamite, is growing up and coming out of that stage now. She is beginning to come to the point where she can give milk and feed others.

The King James Version has a particularly difficult passage in Second Corinthians:

> "Ye are not straitened [cramped, limited, restricted] in us, but ye are straitened in your own bowels.
>
> "Now for a recompence in the same, (I speak as unto my children,) be ye also enlarged [in your own affections, or your will, mind, and emotions]."
>
>   (2 Corinthians 6:12-13, parenthetical insertions mine)

The Message Bible expands our understanding of this passage even more:

THE MAKING OF A BRIDE

*"We didn't fence you in. **The smallness you feel comes from within you. Your lives aren't small, but you're living them in a small way.** I'm speaking as plainly as I can and with great affection. Open up your lives. Live openly and expansively!"*
(2 Corinthians 6:12b-13, MSG, emphasis mine)

The Beloved is enlarging her capacity now not only to "incarnate" the Word, but then to give it out.

God calls Himself "El Shaddai," which you may already know means "the many-breasted one." In other words, He can nurse us all and never run dry. That's El Shaddai.

Several characteristics of the new creature in Christ given by Paul are prefigured here.

Paul knew the Song of Solomon and reflected it in his writings.

"Now therefore ye [Gentiles or non-Jewish people] are no more strangers and foreigners, but fellow citizens with the saints, and of the household of God;

"And are built upon the foundation of the apostles and prophets, Jesus Christ himself being the chief corner stone;

"In whom all the building fitly framed together groweth unto an holy temple in the Lord:

"In whom **ye also are builded together for an habitation of God through the Spirit.**"
(Ephesians 2:19-22, emphasis and insertions mine)

Conybeare and Howson said of Paul's purpose in writing verse 22 above, "He says, 'The soul is a temple of the Holy Spirit; built to make a house wherein God may dwell by the presence of the Spirit.'"

CHAPTER 14 – THE NEW CREATION IN CHRIST

Now, because of Christ's work on the Cross, God's Spirit dwells within our spirit, in our inner being.

Based on our insights into the work of the Spirit in Solomon's stairs of maturity in the Song, you could write in there, *"dove's eyes."* [1]

So build up your life that God may dwell there. Look at Him. Concentrate and focus on Him. Then you will become a reflection of Him.

As the little chorus says:

"I was born to be Your dwelling place,
a home for the presence of the Lord;
so let my life now be consecrated, Lord, to Thee
that I might be what I was born to be."
(source unknown).

I want you to see the Shulamite coming up out of the wilderness. This is how He describes her:

"Behold, you are fair, my love!
"Behold, you are fair!
"You have dove's eyes behind your veil.
"Your hair is like a flock of goats,
Going down from Mount Gilead.
"Your teeth are like a flock of shorn sheep
Which have come up from the washing,
Every one of which bears twins,
And none is barren among them.
"Your lips are like a strand of scarlet,
And your mouth is lovely.

THE MAKING OF A BRIDE

> *"Your temples behind your veil*
> *Are like a piece of pomegranate.*
> *"Your neck is like the tower of David,*
> *Built for an armory,*
> *On which hang a thousand bucklers,*
> *All shields of mighty men.*
> *"Your two breasts are like two fawns,*
> *Twins of a gazelle,*
> *Which feed among the lilies."*
> (Song of Solomon 4:1-5, NKJV, insertion mine).

When you look at this transfigured one coming up out of the wilderness, what do you see in her eyes? You see Him, not her.

You can tell a lot by looking people straight in the eye. You can learn much about their lives, values, character, and past experiences.

When you look at her, what do you see? You see Him.

When the Beloved looks at her, He says that her hair is like fine, silky goat's hair (Song of Solomon 4:1). This represents her strength of character and personhood in Him.

You get an even clearer sense of her strength of character if you keep looking.

The Beloved points out that her brilliantly white teeth are like a flock of newly shorn and washed ewes coming up from the riverbank.

Again, this represents her great capacity to incarnate truth and the Word (much as we use our teeth to "masticate" our food for proper digestion) and make it a part of her life and to minister to others. This is a great description. I hope it fits you.

CHAPTER 14 – THE NEW CREATION IN CHRIST

Her lips are scarlet because they're blood washed, and her speech is appropriate and fitting and not biting, cutting, nasty or vile.

Her temples are like pomegranate. That is, her thoughts are translucent and transparent, gentle, and "safe" because they are tinged with blood.

They resemble the scarlet of the pomegranate because they are "blood-washed" thoughts, reflecting motives that are pure and clean, kept safely behind a veil of modesty and self-effacement.

Her neck is like a strong tower, offering safe storage of all weapons of defense, and secure rest for the soul because she will not cause harm or betray.

He says her breasts are beginning to mature because she's been feeding among the lilies (she is described *as* a lily at one point in the Song).

She's been feeding in the church with the congregation and she is growing. She doesn't say, "I can't ever get fed—I need to find another church." No, she developed her own teeth to feed among the lilies so she could become a feeder herself.

(You need to develop *yourself* so that others can come and draw from you their life as well.)

Paul again reflects the vivid portrait in the Song in Ephesians 3:

> *"[I bow my knees] that He would grant you, according to the riches of His glory,* **to be strengthened with might by his Spirit** *in the inner man."*
> (Ephesians 3:16, emphasis and insertion from v. 14a mine)

THE MAKING OF A BRIDE

The soul is "strengthened with might by the Spirit in the inner man" *so that we are able to walk in high places with Christ Jesus.*

This is an allusion to the "hind's feet" mentioned in the Old Testament. It relates to our ability to walk "the secret places of the Stairs" with our Beloved.

> *"He maketh my feet like hinds' feet, and setteth me upon my high places."* (Psalm 18:33)

> *"The Lord God is my strength, and He will make my feet like hinds' feet, and He will make me to walk upon mine high places."* (Habakkuk 3:19)

Since we are talking about hind's feet and their ability to walk upon the "high places," do you remember the goats from Mount Gilead with the beautiful hair?

They live among the mountain streams and freely roam the sheer mountainsides feeding and drinking freely to mature and possess strength.

If you apply this as a spiritual metaphor, then they have developed the teeth and appetite to "masticate the Word" and drink deeply from the streams of the Spirit of God as they follow Him freely and without coercion.

Paul put it this way:

> *"And have put on the new man, which is **renewed in knowledge** after the image of Him that created him."* (Colossians 3:10)

The mind is renewed in knowledge. Think of Solomon's reference to the shorn sheep as resembling "teeth."

CHAPTER 14 – THE NEW CREATION IN CHRIST

Proverbs 15:7 tells us that the lips of the wise are purged and yielded to God at His utterance. That speaks of the Shulamite's *"scarlet lips"* (Song of Solomon 4:3).

The humble, modest mind of the Bride is reflected in the pomegranate within the veil.

Steadfast, trustworthy character is revealed in her neck, compared to David's tower.

Her growing capacity for the strong meat of the Word is pictured by her breasts; compared to two fawns feeding among the lilies.

All of the things that are in this book emerge in the writings of the *New Testament*, but you have to know this book in order to see them. When they come into focus, you can say, "Oh, Paul or Peter got that from the Song."

Then, if you are reading in the *Old Testament*, you may find yourself exclaiming, "Oh, now I see where the Song drew that from."

It's wonderful, but we still have two more steps to go. Yet, through the whole process we have this incredible promise from One who Himself is truth:

"If any man be in Christ, he is a new creation. Old things are passed away; behold, all things are become new."
(2 Corinthians 5:17 ERV, marginal notes)

THE MAKING OF A BRIDE

End Notes - Chapter 14

1. See Chapter 7, Dove *(Devoted in the Banqueting House)*, where we examine the fifth step of the Stairs, "Communion With Him." Devoted worship produces a special level of intimacy that only occurs when we come together with the Holy Spirit of God. At this stage, the Beloved told the Shulamite woman, "Thou hast dove's eyes" (Song 1:15).

CHAPTER 15

STAIRSTEP 11
SEATED IN THE HEAVENS WITH HIM

ENTHRONED AND ESTABLISHED

SONG OF SOLOMON 4:6-8

"We which live are always delivered unto death...that the life also of Jesus may be manifested in our mortal flesh."
(2 Corinthians 4:11)

THE RESURRECTION SIDE OF THE CROSS

"Until the day be cool, and the shadows flee away, I will get me to the mountain of myrrh, and to the hill of frankincense."
(Song of Solomon 4:6)

The Beloved is speaking to the Shulamite.

She is now seated in the heavenlies with the Beloved in a place of revelation and intimacy.

She's in Him. Now He is saying to her, "I am going to dwell in the mountain of myrrh and the hill of frankincense." Myrrh speaks of death to self, and frankincense has represented brokenness for generations.

She may be tempted to think that the shadows of doubt and disappointment are over in such a sweet place.

It is true on the God-ward side that He has conquered doubt and disappointment. He actually conquered those before the beginning from His point of view. [1]

He cast all of our sins into the sea of forgetfulness at this point, and He never looks at us at any of these stages except as though we were Christ.[2] He sees our possibilities, not just our problems. He even sees our problems *in terms of* our possibilities. We don't, but He does.

But on the man-ward side, her Beloved must now take her down the path of knowing Him *in the fellowship of His suffering* to bring her into the resurrected life.

> *"The shadows must deepen until His appearing, when at evening time there shall be light."*   **(Zechariah 14:7)**

Did you catch that? The shadows have got to deepen until it is evening or dark. Then comes the promise: we'll have light even in the darkest place!

She learns that she can truly have the Resurrected Life only through the knowledge/experience of the *Cross*.

The manifestation of his life depends upon resting upon and assimilating His *death*.

His death? (This is going to get absolutely exquisite.)

Where does He live? He lives on the *mountain of myrrh* and the *hill of frankincense*. Remember that myrrh represents death to self, and being alive to God.

CHAPTER 15 - ENTHRONED AND ESTABLISHED

Jesus perfectly illustrated this in His very real human life when He prayed to His Father in the Garden just before His arrest and crucifixion, "Not my will, Lord, but thine be done."

Paul did the same when he wrote:

> "***I am crucified*** with Christ: nevertheless ***I live***; yet not I, but Christ liveth in me: and the life which I now live in the flesh I live by the faith of the Son of God, who loved me, and gave himself for me." (Galatians 2:20, emphasis mine)

The mountain of *myrrh* is *death* to self and to pride.

This is where our Lord lives and has His being.

I have news for you: He wants us to live there with Him.

If myrrh represents death to self and being alive in God, what is the hill of *frankincense*? It is *Calvary*, which represents brokenness, vulnerability and trust.

Jesus was broken for us, but first He answered His Father's most costly request in the Garden with obedience in *absolute trust* when He said, "Not my will but Thine be done."

Even in death, He trusted His Father. Indeed, with His last breath on the Cross, He cried, "Father, into Thy hands I commend my spirit" (Luke 23:46).

The life in union with the Beloved will often go to the place called *Calvary*.

*Until the Day of Grace is past, all sin and uncleanness will be dealt with **only** at Calvary.*

Even in the "heavenlies" of union with God, He says to His own, "I will get me to the mountain of myrrh–to the hill of frankincense." This is selflessness. He leads the way by example first, and then He expects us to follow Him in selflessness as well.

God doesn't want to break us down, but He wants vulnerability and brokenness before Him to characterize everything about our lives. Then He can live His life through us and make us "more than conquerors."

He is the *Magnet* Who draws her along this path of more and more perfect union with Himself.

There is a big difference between being *a friend* of God and being *in union* with God. This "path of more and more perfect union with Him" is the path walked by the bride-in-progress.

The virgins also start out walking along that path, but they soon fall away. Some of them still live on the first step of the stair, loving the peace they've found there as a friend of the Groom. Others move to the second step and remain there, still looking for more blessings.

Most of us understand that, don't we? Some of them live on the third stair, somehow remaining hungry but never satisfied. For this reason, this group of virgins tends to run from meeting to meeting and church to church. They may attend as many as 20 churches in their lifetime, always looking for the "right one."

Some of the virgins make it all the way to the sixth or even the tenth step of the stairs. Each of these steps is a great place to be in the journey of discipleship and maturity, but not as a permanent dwelling place at the cost of stopping short of becoming a bride!

You go to heaven from any one of these steps, but God wants us to follow Him to the top, so we can become the bride.

CHAPTER 15 – ENTHRONED AND ESTABLISHED

Remember that He is the master teacher, the *perfect teacher guide* described by my former mentor, Dr. Earl V. Pullias. And He likes to reveal Himself at the very place where He wishes to draw His bride.

He will give answers and blessings in due time—but *first* He wants her to come to *Him*. He wants her to choose *HIM* by faith—not the answer, and not the blessing—she needs to choose *Him*.

As she chooses Him *alone*, she becomes more and more "conformed to His image."

THE OUTLOOK IN THE HEAVENLIES

"Thou art all fair, My love…Come with Me…My bride: look from the top…from the lions' dens." (Song of Solomon 4:7–8)

The Bridegroom is speaking, "Thou art all fair, my love. Come with me, my bride." Carefully consider his next words: "Look from the top, from the lions' dens."

He calls her His *bride* for the first time—declaring her union with Him.

This is the place where He calls her His bride for the *first time*, declaring her union with Him. He calls her "bride" at this point because He is calling her *to become what He has chosen her to be.*

She is not yet the crowned spouse, but He is calling her into His will and purpose for her. This is the way God works, isn't it? At every stage along the line, we've seen Him go to the next stage of development and call her to Him there.

He says, "Come with me."

THE MAKING OF A BRIDE

Remember that earlier He said, "Come away—forget those things which are behind and press toward the high calling."

At this point, He was saying, "Come with Me. Forget those things which are behind and come with me."

Paul the apostle told the Philippian disciples, "…this one thing I do, forgetting those things which are behind, and reaching forth unto those things which are before, I press toward the mark for the prize of the high calling of God in Christ Jesus" (Philippians 3:13-14).

Now the Beloved can say, "Come *with* Me," because she is inwardly and outwardly in *union* with Him at this point in her life.

Something wonderful takes place at this stage. He gives her a brand new perspective and paradigm, a new view of things at this point.

He instructs her to "look from the *top*."

> "*Thou art all fair, my love; there is no spot in thee.*
>
> "**Come with me** *from Lebanon, my spouse, with me from Lebanon:* **look from the top** *of Amana, from the top of Shenir and Hermon, from the lions' dens, from the mountains of the leopards.*"   (Song of Solomon 4:7–8)

Now she can see as He sees, with *His* values and His *perspective*!

For many years in three corporate entities: Beacon University, Christian Life School of Theology (CLST), and TEC, a publishing company, I appointed a president over each company. Then I set things up so that when I was away, my wife was still in charge.

Do you know why? It is simple: I told each of the corporate presidents to go to my wife to confirm and corroborate their actions

CHAPTER 15 – ENTHRONED AND ESTABLISHED

because she had my perspective. She knew what I would do if I were there. Frankly, each of those presidents also knew what I would do in most cases, but they were careful to corroborate and confirm things with her.

I didn't establish my wife as the "go-to" person because she was the dominant leader or a dictator; and I didn't do it because I thought the others were untrustworthy. No, I did it because she knew my perspective.

The Lord wants us to know His perspective too. He wants us to see things as He does, and to have His values and perspective on life.

The Beloved has asked the Shulamite to look from the *top*. Now, *she is walking in His victory* and walking "in His shoes." She is becoming His representative and ambassador.

From the moment she said, "I will arise" (Song of Solomon 3:1–2), she has been so preoccupied with *Him* that there are no words about herself, her holiness, her ministry.

If you remember, the Shulamite tended to talk too much in the first two chapters. The endless chatter, the self-absorption, and the repetitive use of I, me, my, and mine are gone from her vocabulary at this point. It's all about *Him*.

- She "passed by all things and *found Him*" (Song of Solomon 3:4).
- She is no longer turned aside by "the *foxes*" (Song of Solomon 2:15).
- When the daughters glorified God in her, she said *nothing* about herself, but quietly walked in His footsteps to do His will.

- When the Beloved called her fair and described her character so fully, she said *nothing* about herself but trusted His Word alone about her.

Now she has come into the new life in union with Him; she is ready to "look from the top" to enjoy the mountain vision.

Notice carefully which mountains the Beloved mentions. As is virtually always the case with the Lord, there is purpose and specific meaning behind each mountain named that goes far beyond mere geography.

He bids her to look from the top of *Amana*.

The name, *Amana*, comes from the Hebrew root, *aman*. It means "truth and integrity," and we get our word *Amen* from it. It describes things that are real and genuine.

The Shulamite doesn't have to pretend anymore. She doesn't have to "fake it until she makes it" anymore. She's *there*.

The Beloved tells her to look at the world from the *top* of The Mountain of Integrity and Confidence. Then she is to deal with people from that vantage point. It means she should not try to impress anybody or make it from somewhere she isn't. He says, "Look from the *top* of The Mountain of Integrity."

He bids her to look from *Shenir*.

Secondly, the Beloved asks her to look from the top of the mountain of Shenir or Senir. Senir is a Hebrew term for a "coat of mail."

Isn't it ironic that Paul the apostle *twice* tells the Bride of Christ, the Church, in the New Testament, "Put on the *whole armor of God*"? (See Ephesians 6:11, 13).

CHAPTER 15 – ENTHRONED AND ESTABLISHED

Now Goliath the giant wore his man-made coat of mail and it didn't do him any good. So did King Saul, with the same result.

David even tried on Saul's armor before battling Goliath, but it wasn't right for him. He went into battle armed with faith in his heart, the Word of God in his mouth, and the commission of God in his hand. He was wearing the whole armor of God.

Whatever you do, and whenever you look out over a spiritual battlefield or the realms of this earth, look from the *top* of the Mountain of the Whole Armor of God. Let Him encase your mind, your will, your emotions, and your physical body with Christ.

He bids her to look from *Hermon*.

Then He bids her look from Hermon. *Hermon*, pronounced "her-mone'" means "sacred." In a sense it means "destruction."

It comes from the Hebrew word, *herem*, which means in this context, to "set apart to God." Our English word harem has its root here. *She is bidden to look from union with Him.*

This means He wants her (and you and me) to look at things from God's Kingdom perspective and values. God has destroyed the works of the devil in our lives (we have *died* and *risen* with Christ to walk in newness of life).

Even through the wilderness experience and the previous steps of the stair, the Beloved has set her apart as sacred and exclusive to Himself. Now, she is far above all principality and power with Him as the King. When the world deals with her, they deal with Him in all of His power and authority.

"The lions' dens" are far beneath His feet so she can "tread upon the young lion and the serpent."

THE MAKING OF A BRIDE

He also mentions the lions' dens that are far beneath His feet. She can now tread upon the young lion and the serpent in Him.

> *"Thou shalt tread upon the lion and adder: the young lion and the dragon shalt thou trample under feet."* (Psalm 91:13)

What are these lions' dens? In this context, they represent demonic expressions of Satan, including the dragon and the lion that seek to destroy.

Now she is raised up so high over them that the God of peace will bruise Satan under her feet as she (representing the Church) learns more and more about how to overcome through the blood of the Lamb.

> *"And they **overcame him by the blood of the Lamb**, and by the word of their testimony; and they loved not their lives unto the death."* (Revelation 12:11, emphasis mine)

> *"I give you power to tread upon serpents and scorpions and over all the power of the enemy."* (Luke 10:19)

Do you see what is happening here? He is giving His bride the keys to the Kingdom, just as He has done for the Church of the Redeemed. He has given us the delegated power from Heaven to "tread on serpents and scorpions and over all of the power of the enemy"!

This is what it means to live from *"above and not beneath,"* and to be *"more than conquerors"* in this life![3] Yes, the Enemy of our souls has power, but you have greater power in union with Him!

It is time to look at every obstacle in front of you in terms of who you are in Him. *Look from the top* and deal with them accordingly!

CHAPTER 15 – ENTHRONED AND ESTABLISHED

End Notes - Ch. 14 – Enthroned & Established

1. This is a metaphor for the God who "sees the end from the beginning" (Isaiah 46:10), and for the Lamb of God who was "slain before the foundation of the world" by God's eternal reckoning (Revelation 13:8).

2. See Micah 7:19.

3. See Deuteronomy 28:13 and John 8:23, where Jesus Himself used these terms in conflict with earthly authority. Also see Romans 8:37 where Paul tells the Church how conquerors deal with the conquered.

THE MAKING OF A BRIDE

CHAPTER 16

STAIRSTEP 12
SERVING OTHERS
WITH HIM

BRIDE AND PARTNER

SONG OF SOLOMON 4:9—5:1

"Blessed be the God and Father of our Lord Jesus Christ, Who hath blessed us with every spiritual blessing in the heavenly places in Christ." (Ephesians 1:3)

THE BLESSINGS IN THE HEAVENLIES

- **The Beloved can now reveal Himself *fully* to His betrothed** as He has been unable to do up to this point of her journey into union.

- **There are *four* major manifestations within her** that He can now share fully. We will take them one at a time.[1] The first of these great revelations that He speaks about her is that she has *the love of the Spirit* in her.

THE MAKING OF A BRIDE

THE LOVE OF THE SPIRIT

*"Thou hast given Me courage, My **sister bride** ... with one look from thine eyes ... **How fair is thy love,** My sister bride! ... Thy lips, O bride, drop honey: honey and milk under thy tongue; and the smell of thy garments is like **the smell of Lebanon."***
(Song of Solomon 4:9–11 ERV, marginal notes, italic emphasis mine)

This verse marks the one instance where the Beloved mentions "the *smell* of Lebanon," although the cedars or trees of Lebanon appear often in the Bible. The majestic trees of Lebanon represent human effort crowned with His presence (as we saw in the "chariot" of the previous chapter). We also see this in the Temple of Solomon adorned with furnishings crafted from the cedars of Lebanon.

The heart of the Beloved is *satisfied* with her.

Every part of the loving language the Beloved uses to describe His bride in verses 9-11 makes it clear that He is *satisfied* with her. And let me say this to you as well: the heart of the Beloved is satisfied with *you* too.

I know that your life (as well as mine) has probably not reached any level we would call perfection. From the man-ward side, we all have some problems, especially in these relational areas.

Most of us are standing solidly within our identity as part of the Bride of Christ, but there are elements in each of our lives that are scattered all along the 12 steps of the stairs of maturity! We are "strewn all over" this mountain of God's grace!

CHAPTER 16 – BRIDE AND PARTNER

Some of us may understand mentally that in the Spirit, we truly are "friends of God," and though we are still hungry for it, we haven't experienced it yet. Even worse, we may "have it" today only to feel we have "lost it" tomorrow.

I may get my victory over my temper one day and then lose it the next. You may get the ability to really get into the Word, and enter into intercession and prayer one week, but then lose it the next.

Sometimes, we have to admit we are not as honest and open as we ought to be. At times, we have things in our lives that we don't want people to know about, so we hide them. In especially honest moments, some of us might even admit that we've been known to lie now and then.

Personally, I may know that in *some* areas I live on *Stairstep 11* or perhaps even *Stairstep 12*, but that isn't enough. I'm really trying to get *all of me* into *all of Him*, with no "loose ends" straggling behind four or six steps down the trail of maturity.

This is where I want to live my life. I'm hungry for that. I want to be everything He wants me to be.

This is the bride life of *The Song of Solomon*. Can you see that *you don't have to be perfect, but hungry*? Remember the attitude revealed in one of Jesus' most remembered and quoted messages to the world?

> *"Blessed are they which do hunger and thirst after righteousness: for they shall be filled."* (Matthew 5:6)

We can have fullness now if we'll just pay the price and "spend that coin of commitment." Yes, the grace of God is free and we can't earn being His friend. However, everything past that point is purchased by *the coin of commitment, surrender, submission and servanthood.*

We see the Beloved's satisfaction with the bride expressed in John's Gospel where Jesus prays His great "high priestly prayer" for the Church that would arise after His death and resurrection:

> *"... that the love wherewith Thou hast loved Me may be in them, and I in them."* (John 17:26b)

Jesus was praying, "Oh God, I want 'everything that they have coming' to fill their lives."

Paul the apostle caught it in the Book of Romans where he said, "...the love of God is shed abroad in our hearts by the Holy Ghost which is given unto us" (Romans 5:5b).

He was picturing divine love being planted like a seed in our hearts. Little by little, that seed grows into a mature plant and then we live off the fruit of that mature plant.

That is God's dream and desire.

"How *fair* is thy love, My sister bride" (Song of Solomon 4:10).

When the Beloved says, "How *fair* is thy love," remember the definition of the Hebrew word translated "fair." It means "transparent, translucent."

So the Beloved is saying, "How *transparent* and *translucent* is thy love, my *sister bride*! Your love is like the Sea of Crystal before the throne." It meant He found nothing hidden, rebellious, or even reluctant in her.

CHAPTER 16 – BRIDE AND PARTNER

"Sister Bride"

"For both He that sanctifieth and they that are sanctified are all of one; for which cause He is not ashamed to call them brethren." (Hebrews 2:11)

Notice the Beloved calls the Shulamite "My sister bride" at this stage. Something has shifted! This is a dramatic change.

Think of all of the transitions we've seen in the Shulamite's life.

First, she was the Shekinah.

Then she became the bed, and then the chariot.

When she walked out of the wilderness, she was transfigured by Him to prepare for their wedding. He said, "If you look at her and look in her eyes, you will see a reflection of Me."

In Song of Solomon Chapter 4 He painted a detailed portrait of her beauty with His words. Her hair is her strength and her lips are scarlet, meaning that her words are blood-washed. And so it went.

He said all of that to prepare her to become His exalted bride. Here at last, He calls her Sister Bride for the first time!

> *"How fair is thy love, **My sister bride**!... Thy lips, O bride, drop honey: honey and milk under thy tongue; and the smell of thy garments is like **the smell of Lebanon**."*
> (Song of Solomon 4:9–11 ERV, marginal notes; italic and bold emphasis mine)

Remember that He is declaring who she is and what He has called her to become. Now, if the Beloved declares these things about her in the Song, then He's declaring that of you and me as His Bride. This is who we are.

THE MAKING OF A BRIDE

Even better, our destiny and calling are to become *one* with Him.

> *"For both he that sanctifieth and they who are sanctified are all of one: for which cause he is not ashamed to call them brethren."*
> (Hebrews 2:11)

Now, who is the one who sanctifies or "sets apart for special service"? Jesus.

And who set them apart? They were set apart in Christ. He is talking about the work of pulling them out of sin, setting them apart, and putting them into righteousness and Kingdom partnership.

Only Jesus can do that.

So *Jesus* who sanctifies, and *we* who are sanctified, are all of One, under One, and out of One. Jesus, the Son of God, *"...is not ashamed to call [us] brethren"* (Hebrews 2:11b).

In other words, Jesus calls us *brother*.

We *also* fit the description the Beloved used for the Shulamite: "My sister bride." That is because we are His "sister in the Father," and "the bride in the Son."

In John 20:17b, Jesus said to Mary Magdalene:

> *"... go to my brethren, and say unto them, I ascend unto **my Father**, and **your Father**; and to **my God**, and **your God**."*
> (John 20:17, emphasis mine)

In Galatians 3:28b, the Apostle Paul summed up our unique and supernatural relationship with Jesus in one sentence:

> *"There is neither Jew nor Greek, there is neither bond nor free, there is neither male nor female: **for ye are all one in Christ Jesus**."* (Galatians 3:28, emphasis mine)

CHAPTER 16 – BRIDE AND PARTNER

She is now so responsive to Him that one *look* is her answer to His every call.

> *"Thou hast given Me courage, My **sister bride...with one look from thine eyes"*...* (Song of Solomon 4:9, ERV, marginal notes, italic emphasis mine)

All they had to do was *look* at each other. The level of response in the Shulamite was even more sensitive than the steeds pulling Pharaoh's celebrated war chariots.

Those horses were so well trained and acclimated to their master that they needed only a slight movement of the bridle. They didn't need to be whipped, gouged or jerked. All it took was a gentle flick of the wrist or subtle move of the charioteer's fingers to trigger an instant response.

The "sister-bride" didn't need even that. He guided her *with His eyes!*

This is like two married people who after fifty years know each other's every thought.

I'll never forget the elderly couple I observed in the restaurant, because what I saw in their relationship was something I later longed for in my own marriage (and in my walk with God).

He wants to lead her onward and "fulfill in her every desire of goodness and every work of faith, with power" (2 Thessalonians 1:11).

> *"Wherefore also we pray always for you, that our God would count you worthy of this calling, and fulfill all the good pleasure of his goodness, and the work of faith with power."*
> (2 Thessalonians 1:11)

She is becoming more and more *fragrant* with the sweetness of His presence, and His love within her "fills her heart" and makes her lips drop words "sweet as honey" and "pure as milk."

After walking with the Lord many decades, I've learned to pray another way.

I don't pray, "Oh, Lord, let me know what to say."

I don't pray, "Oh, Lord, let me do the right thing."

Now I pray, "Lord, let me exude Your presence. When I'm there, let people be aware that You are there."

I make sure I don't pray, "Oh, God, what can I do to impress these people, what can I do . . . ? "

No, I simply pray, "Lord, let them be aware of You when they are looking at and talking to me."

It reminds me of a **Persian fable** that I learned when I was a very young man. I've never forgotten it. Now I want to pass it on to you:

A Persian fable: "Those Who Dwell With Sharon's Rose"

"One day
A wanderer found a lump of clay.
So redolent of sweet perfume,
Its odors lightened up the room.
'What art thou?' was his quick demand.
'Art thou some gem from Samarcand?'
'Or spikenard in rude disguise,
'Or other costly merchandise?'
Nay, I am but a lump of clay!
'Then, whence this wondrous perfume, say?'

CHAPTER 16 – BRIDE AND PARTNER

> 'Friend, if my secret I disclose,
> I have been dwelling with the Rose.'"
> Ah, sweet parable—and will not those
> Who dwell with Sharon's Rose
> Distill sweet odors all around
> Though low and mean themselves are found?"

I love this poetic fable because it describes what the mystery of "God in us" is all about. His plan all along has been to plant in our hearts the love of the Spirit.

Our job is to let people sense the love of the Spirit. The Bride is God's tangible presence in the world.

My hope is that as you read this poem, and as you read and study The Song of Solomon, that every one of those metaphors will carry a deep revelation for you.

THE *FRUIT* OF THE SPIRIT

> "A garden barred is My sister bride; a **spring shut up**, a **fountain sealed.** Thy shoots are a **paradise** with precious fruits…with all trees of frankincense … with all the chief spices."
> (Song of Solomon 4:12–14 ERV, marginal notes, emphasis mine)

The Beloved likens His redeemed one to a *garden enclosed* for Himself alone.

I met the late Dr. Sam Sasser many years ago when he preached a message based on this passage entitled, "A Fountain Sealed." I was amazed to hear this great saint and church leader define and describe the Bride from the Song of Solomon.

THE MAKING OF A BRIDE

The Beloved likens His redeemed to a garden enclosed. A *garden enclosed* for Himself alone.

He compares her to a prepared garden. Understand that is *not* something growing wild or spontaneously. Godliness doesn't grow wild. It only grows under the disciplining hand of a gardener. It requires a great deal of landscaping, fertilizing, pruning, and cutting to produce the wide variety of things found in a prized enclosed garden.

Randy Alcorn wrote a book entitled, *Heaven*, in 2004. Within the 500 pages of this well-researched book, he defined the original word translated as "paradise" in this passage from the Song and noted that it comes from the Persian word, *pairidaeza*. It means "a walled park or an enclosed garden."[2]

The Beloved is saying here, "Sister Bride, you are a paradise on earth. Everything the world needs to come into right relationship with Me, with God, is inside of you."

Isn't that true for the Church and of the Bride of Christ? To a certain extent, it is true of every child of God!

She is wholly under His Lordship to fulfill His will and pleasure.

Alcorn went on to say, "Paradise does not refer to wild nature but to nature under mankind's dominion." And in this context, to *human life* under *God's* control and dominion.

John 15 captures it in Jesus' words to His disciples:

> *"Ye have not chosen me, but I have chosen you, and ordained you, that ye should go and bring forth fruit, and that your fruit should remain: that whatsoever ye shall ask of the Father in my name, he may give it you."* (John 15:16)

CHAPTER 16 – BRIDE AND PARTNER

She brings forth *fruit*.

What is the fruit of the Spirit? Paul the apostle tells us in his letter to the Galatians:

> *"But the fruit of the Spirit is love, joy, peace, longsuffering, gentleness, goodness, faith, meekness, temperance: against such there is no law."* (Galatians 5:22–23)

These virtues are godly fruit of a life lived for and with God in the "garden" of our lives. It grows naturally when we allow ourselves to be led by the Spirit rather by our fleshly nature. The Bible says, "For as many as are led by the Spirit of God, they are the sons [*huioi*, heirs and joint-heirs] of God" (Romans 8:14, parenthetical insertion mine).

She brings forth *much* fruit.

> *"Herein is my Father glorified, that ye bear much fruit; so shall ye be my disciples."*
> (John 15:8)

THE EVIDENCE THAT WE ARE DISCIPLES ... BRINGING FORTH MUCH FRUIT.

Jesus says His Father is glorified when we bear *much* fruit. In fact, He goes on to say that *much fruit* is evidence that we are His disciples (or "disciplined ones").

This is a picture of the Shulamite totally under His authority, disciplined by His wonderful hand, and bearing *much fruit*.

Her *desolation* becomes like a garden of fruit.

> *"And they shall say, This land that was desolate is become **like the garden of Eden; and the waste and desolate and** ruined cities are become fenced, and are inhabited."*
> (Ezekiel 36:35, emphasis mine)

THE MAKING OF A BRIDE

The Shulamite's desolation transforms to delight in the presence of the King. In His presence, His fullness overcame her lack when she was hurting, wounded, or felt alone.

They shall see that the Lord has done it.

> "I will open rivers in high places, and fountains in the midst of the valleys: I will make the wilderness a pool of water, and the dry land springs of water.
>
> "I will plant in the wilderness the cedar, the shittah tree, and the myrtle, and the oil tree [the olive tree]; I will set in the desert the fir tree, and the pine, and the box tree together:
>
> "That they may see, and know, and consider, and understand together, that **the hand of the Lord hath done this,** and the Holy One of Israel hath created it." (Isaiah 41:18–20)

These verses from Isaiah 41 are so beautiful. Apply them to the Shulamite who became one with the Beloved.

The richer the bride is with all of the things of the Spirit, and all of the things that make for a fullness of life, the more people know that God alone did it, not her. All of the glory goes to God.

THE LIVING *WATER* OF THE SPIRIT

> "Thou art a fountain of gardens, a well of living waters, and flowing streams." (Song of Solomon 4:15)

The Beloved declared that His "sister bride" was "a barred or a walled garden" in verse 12. This demonstrates the love and fruit of the Spirit in her life.

Then He says in verse 15, "You are a *fountain* of gardens, a *well* of *living waters* and *flowing streams.*"

CHAPTER 16 – BRIDE AND PARTNER

Remember that the Beloved is describing His bride and her *union* with Him. Consider these *metaphors* as you draw out their revelatory meaning: the *love* of the Spirit, the *fruit* of the Spirit, and now the *living water* of the Spirit.

The Beloved makes her a "shut up spring," a "fountain sealed" so that *He* is the Source of her "flowing streams" (Song of Solomon 4:12).

If sewage or a chemical contaminant pollutes a flowing stream, then the water is undrinkable at any point down stream from that entry of pollution.

She is a "spring shut up" for Him alone—a pure spring.

The Beloved calls His bride a "shut up spring" and a "fountain sealed" as a way to show there can be no pollution coming into it. In this way, only a pure spring of living water flows from that artesian well.

He guards the soul so that its waters are not *polluted* by its own carnal or natural self, or by the will of others.

He is the Supreme and Sole Possessor of the waters of her soul (that which flows out.)

He determines what flows out of her by determining what flows into her.

The Beloved makes her a *fountain* of living water—a living spring.

This is reflected in John 4 where Jesus draws a metaphorical picture of limitless spiritual water in a fallen world known for its spiritual drought and desolation:

"But whosoever drinketh of the water that I shall give him shall never thirst; but the water that I shall give him shall be in him a well of water springing up into everlasting life." (John 4:14)

"He that believeth on me, as the scripture hath said, out of his belly shall flow rivers of living water." (John 7:38)

The Beloved makes her a *flowing stream*.

Two conditions **only are required for this pure and living spring to become a flowing stream for others.**

Number one, we must continuously *abide* in Him.

Let me show you something in John 7:38. We quoted the King James Version earlier: "He that believeth on me, as the scripture hath said, out of his belly shall flow rivers of living water."

The opening phrase in verse 38, "He that believeth *on* me ..." is not a good translation. A better reading would be, "He that believeth *eis*, or *'into'* me...."

The Greek term used here means "belief *into* Him," not belief *on* or *about* Him. We are to trust *into* Him, so that the more you trust then the more you are *in* the cleft of the Rock. That is the whole idea. At *that* point, it can be said, "Out of your inner most being, then, will flow living water."

Number two, we must be *willing* to be poured out or unsealed so that others may be blessed.

I love to preach from a passage in 2 Kings, Chapter 4. In case you are not familiar with this incident in the ministry of Elisha the prophet, I urge you to read it before moving on in this book:

CHAPTER 16 – BRIDE AND PARTNER

"And Elisha said unto her, 'What shall I do for thee? tell me, what hast thou in the house?' And she said, 'Thine handmaid hath not anything in the house, save a pot of oil.'

"Then he said, 'Go, borrow thee vessels abroad of all thy neighbours, even empty vessels; borrow not a few.

"And when thou art come in, thou shalt shut the door upon thee and upon thy sons, and shalt pour out into all those vessels, and thou shalt set aside that which is full.'

"So she went from him, and shut the door upon her and upon her sons, who brought the vessels to her; and she poured out.

"And it came to pass, when the vessels were full, that she said unto her son, 'Bring me yet a vessel.' And he said unto her, 'There is not a vessel more.' And the oil stayed.

"Then she came and told the man of God. And he said, 'Go, sell the oil, and pay thy debt, and live thou and thy children of the rest.'" (2 Kings 4:2–7)

This woman was a widow with two children. She came to Elisha the prophet because creditors showed up on her doorstep and tried to take her two children as indentured or bonded slaves to pay a debt left after the woman's husband died.

She ran to the man of God (not a bad thing to do), and he responded, "What shall I do for you? Tell me, what hast thou in the house?"

Now, that's the question. Whatever is inside of you is what will flow out of you. The widow's answer was simple: "Thy handmaiden hath not anything in the house except a pot of oil."

Then the prophet told the distressed widow, "Go borrow vessels from your neighbors. Empty vessels, not a few." That reminds me of an old gospel song entitled, "Bring Your Vessels, Not A Few,"

THE MAKING OF A BRIDE

that song is older than most of the folks reading this book. The refrain says:

> He will fill your heart today to overflowing.
> As the Lord commandeth you,
> "Bring your vessels, not a few."
>
> He will fill your heart today to overflowing
> *With the Holy Ghost and power.*[3]

That's the way it is when God calls you to the ministry. Your job is to pour out upon others whatever God gives you. His part is to faithfully keep giving you more than you can give away. You can apply this principle to everything.

WHEN YOU POUR OUT WHAT GOD GIVES YOU ... HE ALWAYS SUPPLIES MORE.

This applies whether God's deposit in your "vessel" is revelation into His Word or purposes, or if it takes the form of finances and money. You can also apply this principle of "giving away" to love, compassion and care. *Whatever* it is, the more of it you give away, then the more He supplies within you!

It all begins with your *willingness* to *abide* and *pour out.*

When she is "walking in Him," she need not worry about the flowing stream. He will bring the needy ones to live and grow from her *overflow*!

This word, overflow, takes me back to when I first started ministering at the age of 14 or 15. As the head of our church youth group, I had to preach to those rascals every week.

CHAPTER 16 – BRIDE AND PARTNER

I started off my ministry with three sermons. The first was from *Genesis* to *Isaiah*, the second was from *Isaiah* to *Malachi*, and the third was from *Matthew* to *Revelation*. That's all I had, and I thought that's all there was.

As I grew up in the Lord and ventured out into the evangelistic field, I constantly looked for good sermons. Anytime I met a good preacher or skilled pastor, I'd say, *"I need a good sermon. Do you have a good sermon you'd let me borrow?"*

For many decades now, I've allowed young people, seminary students, and young ministers to drop by and raid my files of sermons and research material (now don't all of you come at once).

They would fill out outlines, photocopy texts, and take copies of entire files with them. At this point, I have spiritual sons and daughters all over the country and the world.

Every month for many years, I've sent them a Bible teaching and a teaching on leadership. At the end of each year, I've bound both sets of materials into books as gifts for them.

And yes, I am truly *blessed* when I hear that they are preaching these messages or have adopted them as their own. I'm constantly told that whenever they are stuck and can't seem to get through a situation, these resources have become lifelines for them. I love that.

Listen, as you enter into more and more union with the Lord, you will come to the place in Him where everything that comes out of you will come from *the overflow* of your *personal abiding in Him*. When that starts to happen, you won't have to pray for the Shekinah. At that point, you *are* the Shekinah. The revelation will simply and naturally flow into you and out of you.

THE MAKING OF A BRIDE

I will never forget the time a great man named Paul Paino complimented me to the point of embarrassment. He said publically, "Cottle says more by accident than most preachers say on purpose when they preach."

That is a good description of "preaching out of the overflow." This was one of the great compliments of my life. I'm not sure I really truly deserved it, especially at that stage of my life. Perhaps he was calling "those things that are not as though they were." In any case, I thank God that now his words are coming to pass.

THE HEAVENLY *WIND* OF THE SPIRIT

"Awake, O North Wind, and come, thou South; blow upon My garden, that the spices thereof may flow out."
(Song of Solomon 4:16a)

At this point, it is very difficult to know who is speaking these words, the Beloved or the Shulamite bride. Neither one addresses the other, but we do know that *whoever* is speaking is making a declaration. I think it is the Shulamite, but it doesn't really matter in this context because they are in union at this point.

The Holy Spirit is likened to "wind" in the Scripture.

*"Then said he unto me, Prophesy unto the wind, prophesy, son of man, and say to the wind, Thus saith the Lord G*OD*; Come from the four winds,* **O breath,** *and breathe upon these slain,* **that they may live."** *(Ezekiel 37:9)*

So He's talking about the characteristics of the bride.

- She has the *love* of the spirit.
- She has the *fruit* of the spirit.

CHAPTER 16 – BRIDE AND PARTNER

- She has the *water* of the spirit.
- And now she has the *wind* of the spirit.

These are the characteristics of her life.

The human spirit is the *temple* of the Holy Spirit.

The Scriptures themselves best establish this truth.

First, Paul said the Holy Spirit actually dwells within us, in our hearts, as "the temple" of God.

> *"Know ye not that ye are the temple of God, and that the Spirit of God dwelleth in you?"* (1 Corinthians 3:16)

Second, Jesus said the Holy Spirit Himself administers the *new birth*.

> *"The wind bloweth where it listeth, and thou hearest the sound thereof, but canst not tell whence it cometh, and whither it goeth: so is every one that is born of the Spirit."* (John 3:8)

Third, the Holy Spirit *cleanses* or purifies the heart.

> *"And God, which knoweth the hearts, bare them witness, giving them [Gentiles] the Holy Ghost, even as he did unto us [Jews];*
>
> *"And put no difference between us and them, purifying their hearts by faith."* (Acts 15:8-9, parenthetic insertions mine)

Fourth, the Holy Spirit *guides* us into all truth.

> *"Howbeit when he, the Spirit of truth, is come, he will guide you into all truth: for he shall not speak of himself; but whatsoever he shall hear, that shall he speak: and he will shew you things to come."* (John 16:13)

Abiding as she now is in the clear light of the heavenly sphere, the Shulamite is ready for the Breath of the Beloved to move upon her and *use* her as never before!

THE MAKING OF A BRIDE

At last, this is the purpose of all of the growing, of the developing, and struggle of the 12 stair steps to maturity and union.

Look closely at the Shulamite's bridal prayer. It is absolutely phenomenal and it ought to be *our* prayer!

> *"Awake, O North Wind; and come, thou South: blow upon My garden that the spices thereof may flow out."*
> (Song of Solomon 4:16a)

What is the north wind in scripture? It is always used to depict adversity of some kind, whether it comes as persecution, pressure, animosity or natural calamity. The south wind typically represents pleasure, ease, or comfort in some form.

PLEASURE AND PLENTY OR PRESSURE AND PERSECUTION ... GOD, I'M IN.

So what is she saying? She's saying it doesn't matter if I'm under pressure and experiencing persecution, or if I am in a season of pleasure and plenty: God, I'm in!

She says, "Bring the cold, icy winds of the north or the hot, sultry winds of the south into my life as Thou wilt. Only let them mix so that the sweet fragrance of my Beloved will be released and flow out for the sake of others and especially for Him."

Stop and think with me for a moment: Isn't this the perfect picture of the *surrendered life*?

The surrendered soul says daily to the Lord, "Whatever happens in my life, Lord—good, bad, ugly, or beautiful; whatever happens, cause all things to work together for Your glory and the blessing of others."

CHAPTER 16 – BRIDE AND PARTNER

THE ATTITUDE OF THE SURRENDERED SOUL

"Let my Beloved come into His garden, and eat His precious fruits." (Song of Solomon 4:16b)

She has now reached another level. At first, she launched nearly every comment with "I or my," and ended it with "me or mine."

Next she progressed to a place where she talked less about "me and mine" and talked more about "us and ours." She would say *"our cedars ... our bed ... our rafters."*

Now, at this level on the stairs, it's all about Him and nothing about her or hers.

Someone asked me a few years ago after my lecture on the twelfth stair, "Are you there?"

I said, "I want to be there. Yes, that's where I want to 'live and move and have my being' because it really is all about Him and not about me."

Yet I quickly admitted that I am not totally, fully there. I am "righteous and blameless" from the God-ward side, of course. However, I am still "a work in progress" on the man-ward side.

There was a time when I was all the way down on the first step of the stair. We all were.

This is what life is all about. The "crucified life" is the inner purpose of life. We must live the crucified life to enter into and live the glorified life.

This is what's it all about—*the stair steps in the cleft of the rock.*

THE MAKING OF A BRIDE

You can't walk these stairs outside of Christ. However, once you step into Christ by faith, the first thing He does is put a hunger in you for more of Him.

As long as that hunger is there, you will have the grace for the ongoing struggle between the deeper life and the shallow life, between the carnal nature and the reborn spirit.

Life is all about conquering our carnal nature and coming into full union with Him. That is life as pictured in the Book of the *Song of Solomon*. It is magnificent!

This is the *first* recorded utterance of the redeemed one since she entered into rest with her Beloved in the heavenlies (Song of Solomon 4:1).

For at least 16 verses, we haven't heard the Shulamite say a word. She was silent until this moment.

She has learned the *silence* of love, and to be still so that He can speak.

The bride has learned to be still so that He can speak. It is because when He speaks, she grows. In fact, she becomes what He calls her.

As long as she's talking, she's not growing. But when she is silent, He "grows her" with His words.

Earlier she could not help but speak of every revelation, every word for she was weak in divine things.

So she was a jabber box.

Now, it's good to give your testimony. But remember, deep waters are still waters. The deeper the waters, the more placid the surface.

CHAPTER 16 – BRIDE AND PARTNER

She needed a *wilderness* experience to strengthen her so that she could know Him and live the "mountain life." (Revelation comes on mountains and hills in Scripture.)

She needed a wilderness experience to strengthen her so that she could know Him and live that mountain life.

Remember that revelation comes on mountains and hills in scripture. Growth comes with valleys. Revelation comes on mountains.

Now she only wants *Him* to be satisfied:

> "Let my Beloved come into His garden, and eat His pleasant fruit." (Song of Solomon 4:16b)

What is the garden? Didn't the Beloved say "My love is a barred garden, an enclosed garden?"

She is the garden. But now she says, "Let my Beloved come and eat His garden."

I'm not mine. Nothing about me is mine. Nothing I hold is mine.

The garden is *His*, not hers. She is the garden, but she is not her own.

Her prayer and every thought are:

"Not my will, but Thine be done."

THE LIFE ABUNDANT

> "I am come into My garden, My sister, My Bride; I have gathered My myrrh ... My spice ... My honeycomb ... My honey ... My wine with My milk. Eat, O friends ... drink abundantly." (Song of Solomon 5:1)

To her prayer that He will use what He has planted and grown in her, the Bridegroom responds quickly—"I am come!"

THE MAKING OF A BRIDE

He accepts her confession that all is His, for He uses the word "*My*" nine times.

And so what does He do? He does what she said.

He gathers and enjoys the precious *fruit* of her life and ministry.

And then He does something else.

Without asking He turns to the *unsatisfied ones* around and invites them to share this rich, sweet abundance of her life and ministry with Him.

"Eat, O friends, drink abundantly of love."

He says, "Hey, everybody, come on, let's eat of her."

Now He is able to look upon the needy multitudes and say, "Give *ye* them to eat."

Isn't this incredible? He has made her *the answer to the hunger of the world*.

Now, that is who the Bride is. And that is the Church!

She is His *wife* in the bed of intimacy.

She is His *warrior*.

She is also His *garden*. She becomes His sustenance for the hungry, the needy, and those hurting around her.

He says, "Eat, O friends; drink, yea, drink abundantly."

He is saying, "Drink your fill of love—of *agape* or the 'God-kind-of-love.'" That characterizes the life of the Bride of Christ.

Notice that He doesn't ask her permission (nor does He ask ours). Do you want expansion in your ministry or wealth? Do

CHAPTER 16 – BRIDE AND PARTNER

you want to see expansion in your ability to love, serve and help others?

Then abide in Him, and be willing to be poured out.

At last the Beloved is able to look on the multitudes and say, "Give ye, them to eat."

This is the story of the *Song of Solomon*.

There are so many variables in the Song that many become lost in the complexity of this book. Understanding comes when you see the Shulamite woman move from friend to bride along the Twelve Stair Steps.

We too, must move onward and upward from a carnal emphasis on *me and mine* to a God-ward emphasis on *us and our*, to finally a spiritually mature emphasis focused solely on *Him and His*.

I pray this book and the truths it shares have been as much a blessing to you as writing it has been to me.

May God bless you as you continue your ascent of spiritual discipleship in *The Making of a Bride* along *The Rock Stairs of The Song of Solomon*.

THE MAKING OF A BRIDE

End Notes – Ch. 16 – Bride and Partner

1. NOTE: In this final chapter I draw very strongly from the work of Jessie Penn-Lewis in *Thy Hidden Ones*. Although her book was published in 1899, the truths she uncovered are timeless and valuable to any sincere disciple of Jesus and student of God's Word. Indeed, this book is a product of the personal revelations God gave me concerning The Song of Solomon after reading Jessie's original work.

2. Randy Alcorn, *Heaven* (Carol Stream, IL: Tyndale House Publishers, 2004), pg. 55.

3. "Bring Your Vessels, Not A Few," by Leila N. Morris, 1912. In the public domain.

ABOUT THE AUTHOR

Dr. Ronald E. Cottle has been serving the body of Christ for more than six decades. He has extensive experience in teaching, pastoring, public speaking, education administration and both radio and television.

He has developed more than one hundred advanced courses of Christian development and biblical training, and has authored more than three dozen books encompassing ministry, leadership, biblical studies, and church development.

Dr. Cottle's teaching style has been called "scholarship on fire" by those who have attended his lectures. It is clear, dynamic and inspirational. His unique style always contains the compassion of a shepherd, the urgency of a prophet and the wisdom of a statesman. His thoughts and counsel are straightforward, dynamic and powerful. His teachings will help today's spiritual leaders and other sincere "thinking Christians" to discover the mystery and the majesty of the Bible.

Dr. Cottle has earned a Bachelor of Arts (A.B.) degree from Florida Southern College, Lakeland, Florida; a Master of Divinity (M.Div.) from Lutheran Theological Seminary, Columbia, South Carolina; and a Doctor of Philosophy (Ph.D.) in Religion from the University of Southern California, Los Angeles. He also earned a Master of Science in Education (M.S.Ed.) and a Doctor of Education (Ed.D.) from U.S.C.